KIDS' EASY-TO-CREATE

Wildlife
Habitats

for small spaces in the city, suburbs & countryside

Emily Stetson

Illustrations by J. Susan Cole Stone

A WILLIAMSON *KIDS CAN!*® BOOK

WILLIAMSON BOOKS
NASHVILLE, TENNESSEE

Library of Congress Cataloging-in-Publication Data

Stetson, Emily, 1957-
    Kids' easy-to-create wildlife habitats for small spaces / Emily Stetson ; illustrations by J. Susan Cole Stone.
        p. cm. — (A williamson kids can! book)
    Includes index.
    ISBN: 0-8249-8665-2 (pbk.)
        1. Wildlife attracting—Juvenile literature. 2. Habitat (Ecology)—Juvenile literature.
I. Title. II. Series

QL59.S74 2004
639.9'2—dc22   2004040871

Kids Can!® series editor: **Susan Williamson**
Project editor: **Vicky Congdon**
Interior design: **Sydney Wright**
Illustrations: **J. Susan Cole Stone**
Cover design and illustration: **Michael Kline**

Published by Williamson Books
An imprint of Ideals Publications
A division of Guideposts
800-586-2572

Printed in the U.S.A. All rights reserved.

10 9 8 7 6 5 4 3 2 1

Kids Can!®, *Little Hands*®, *Quick Starts for Kids!*®, *Kaleidoscope Kids*®, and *Tales Alive!*® are registered trademarks of Ideals Publications, a division of Guideposts.

Williamson's *Good Times*™ Books, *Little Hands* Story Corners™, and *Quick Starts Tips!*™ are trademarks of Ideals Publications, a division of Guideposts.

Dedication

To my daughters, Erin, Laura, and Annie, with whom I'm able to observe the wonders of nature anew. May you always follow your curiosity and act on your concern for every living creature! And in memory of my mother-in-law, Edie Jackson, who devoted her life to protecting our natural environment.

Acknowledgments

This book was possible only with the hard work, creative expertise, and energy of many dedicated and talented individuals. I am especially grateful to editorial director Susan Williamson for providing the vision and offering encouragement and guidance; to editor (and longtime friend) Vicky Congdon for orchestrating the process and shaping the manuscript into a workable whole; and to proofreader Jean Silveira for her unerring eye for detail and accuracy.

Thanks also to Williamson Books authors Vicky Congdon, Robyn Haus, Susan Milord, Lynn M. Rosenblatt, Warner Shedd, and Susan Williamson for sharing their enthusiasm and ideas with all of us, and to the National Gardening Association, the National Wildlife Federation, and the Vermont Institute of Natural Science for their excellent resources (for more resources, see pages 121 to 123).

Special thanks to Sydney Wright for capturing the essence of the book in her wonderful interior design; to J. Susan Cole Stone for her amazingly life-like wildlife illustrations (you make the pages come alive!); and to Michael Kline for adding his trademark humor to the cover design and illustrations. Thank you all!

Permission is granted by Williamson Books to use limited material or suggestions previously published in *Garden Fun!*, *The Kids' Nature Book*, *The Kids' Wildlife Book*, *Make Your Own Birdhouses & Feeders*, *Monarch Magic!*, and *Summer Fun!*

Contents

Kids & Wildlife Welcome Here!

Wildlife, Habitats & YOU!

This book is for kids everywhere — in the city, the suburbs, and out in the country. You don't have to have a big yard, or even any yard at all, to make a welcoming place for wildlife. Everywhere I've lived — in apartments and rowhouses, in the suburbs, and in more rural spots — I've discovered that it's the simple things you do for wild creatures that can be the most rewarding — and fun!

I grew up in a suburban neighborhood with a postage stamp-sized backyard, bordered by neighbors on either side. But for me and my friends, that tiny yard was our special retreat. We'd search out toads in the cool, moist hiding spots under bushes; watch caterpillars crawl on the concrete; dig up worms and grubs; giggle at the antics of the chipmunks as they scurried along the woodpile; and pick dandelions by the dozens. It was in that tiny yard that I started my first garden — one pumpkin vine and two tomato plants.

What I never really thought about then was how we were actually helping the wildlife around us. Our bird feeders provided resting spots for the migrating songbirds passing through as well as meals for the birds spending the winter with us. The woodpile (and my tiny garden!) created homes for insects, earthworms, and salamanders; our hanging baskets of flowers and even those dandelions were also part of our backyard wildlife habitat.

There are all sorts of ways *you* can help wild critters right where you are, too. Planting a pot of nectar-rich flowers for bees and butterflies, creating a shady retreat for a toad, or even just setting out a log and some bark mulch as an insect refuge may seem like tiny steps. But when lots of kids do a little here and there to create places for wildlife, it all adds up. Working together at a school or other community site, or each of us individually at home, we can make a big difference in the lives of the critters around us. And *that* is something to be proud of!

A Place to Call Home

If someone asked you about the creatures you share your home with, what would you say? There's your family, of course, and perhaps a pet or two, maybe a dog or hamster. But what about the birds that fly around your yard, the insects that buzz past your windows, and the beetles and ants busy in the soil around the tree at the edge of the sidewalk? And don't forget that squirrel you often hear chattering in the trees! Maybe you've come across a toad staying cool in a shady retreat in your yard or spied a snake or lizard sunning itself on a rock. Surprise! There are wild critters all around you that also call where you live "home"!

Each animal, including you, has its own *habitat* — that particular combination of food, shelter, water, and protected space it needs to complete its life cycle. Your surroundings offer all of those things to more animals than you might realize! So, let's explore your yard to determine who's visiting and why. Once you learn what makes your outdoor environment an appealing place to wildlife, you can offer more of it. Think of it as hanging out the wildlife welcome signs!

Whose Habitat Is This, Anyway?

Exactly whose habitat *do* you share? Stop, look, and listen to find out! The first step toward creating a place more critters can call home is to know who already likes being your "neighbor." Some animals will be easy to spot. Even though there will be many you won't see up close, you can look for signs that they have visited. Just think like a detective!

Be a Super Sleuth!

Do you sometimes know who is at your house, even before you see the person? Let's say you get home from school and see a car in the driveway or a briefcase next to the door as you come in. You know your mom is home from work, so you call out, "Hi, Mom!" before you even see her. Or, you see a gym bag plopped down in a chair, notice that the bread bag is wide open, and see a knife stuck into an open jar of peanut butter. You know your older brother is home from practice (and he's hungry!).

By observing these clues, a good detective can draw conclusions about the people around her. And it's the same with noticing animals, too. If you know *where* to look, or *what* to look or listen for, you can often tell who is around, or who has been there recently, without even seeing the animal!

BARN SWALLOWS NESTING IN THE RAFTERS

I Spy ...

Try some wildlife sleuthing right in your yard or around your neighborhood to investigate what animals live there. Here are some tips to help you sharpen your detective skills.

Search up high and down low. Are there any nests overhead in the eaves or in trees? Birds roosting on the tops of buildings or on utility lines? Droppings or feathers on the ground?

Look *closely*. Look carefully at the trunks of trees — what signs might you see that an animal has climbed up to its home in the branches or to escape from a predator? What might tell you that a hungry critter has visited some of the plants in your garden?

Think big and small. Larger animals like squirrels and rabbits are often easy to spot, but keep on the lookout for your smaller animal friends as well. Look under rocks and between sidewalk cracks for all kinds of crawling insects. Butterflies and moths love to land on flowering plants. Intricate webs between bushes, on fenceposts, or in porch corners are a sure sign of spiders. Maybe you'll even be lucky enough to see a beautiful dragonfly with shimmering wings!

TWO-SPOTTED LADYBIRD (LADYBUG)

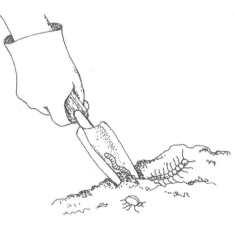

BEETLES AND THE MULTI-LEGGED CENTIPEDE LOVE MOIST SOIL

Dig a little deeper. Ask permission to dig in the garden (if you have one) or in a patch of dirt by your house or apartment building. Critters crawling in the soil are part of what lives around you, too!

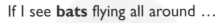

If I see **bats** flying all around …

then I'll guess that **mosquitoes** are out.

BROWN BAT

If I hear **birds singing** …

then I'll look for **nests in trees or eaves** or for **birds roosting** on utility lines.

If I hear **tap, tap, tap** …

then I'll look for a **woodpecker** nearby. I'll also look for grubs and beetles in the tree bark, which the woodpecker might be eating!

WHITE-THROATED SPARROW

DOWNY WOODPECKER

Play "If …, Then …"

See if you can guess what animals might be around with these clues!

If I see **acorns and other nuts** gathered in a pile or I find them buried in the soil …

then I'll look for **squirrels** or other critters burying or hoarding their winter's food.

ALPINE CHIPMUNK

If I see **ants** scurrying in a line …

then I'll look for an **anthill** (or for crumbs in the grass!) nearby.

If I see **paw prints in the mud** or on the sidewalk …

then a **dog, cat, or wild critter** passed by (for more on tracks, see HOT ON THE TRAIL, page 10).

8

Kids' Easy-to-Create Wildlife Habitats

If there's a **web** in the corner of the porch or suspended between two shrubs ...

then I'll look for a **spider**.

GARDEN SPIDER

If I hear a **garbage can** being tipped over in the middle of the night ...

then I'll look for tracks of **raccoons** or other nighttime critters.

NUTTALL'S COTTONTAIL

If **clover and grass** have been nibbled ...

then I'll look for **rabbits** and other wild critters stopping by for a snack.

If the **bark at the base of young trees** is eaten ...

then I'll look for **mice** and other rodents or for **holes in the trunk** that might lead to their nests.

A Wildlife Sleuthing Kit

Did you notice how much you use all of your senses — especially smelling, listening, and seeing — while being a wildlife sleuth? Those are your most important tools for figuring out wildlife clues! Here are a few other items that can also help make your wildlife watching easier.

- ✱ A hand lens or magnifying glass
- ✱ Binoculars
- ✱ Plastic zip-locking bags for collecting things
- ✱ A sketchbook, notebook, or scrapbook (see START A WILDLIFE SCRAPBOOK, page 29)
- ✱ Colored pencils for drawing
- ✱ A field guide to animals or birds in your area (see Resources, page 122)
- ✱ A guide to animal tracks and a ruler (to measure the size of the tracks and the distance between them)
- ✱ A trowel or large spoon for digging
- ✱ A flashlight, for nighttime viewing
- ✱ A bug net (optional; pages 112 to 113)
- ✱ A camera to record your wildlife sightings!

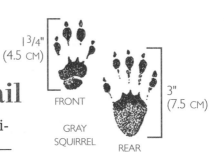

1/2"
(1 CM)

FRONT

3"
(7.5 CM)

3 3/4"
(9.5 CM)

RACCOON

REAR

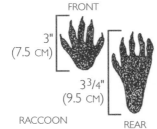

1 3/4"
(4.5 CM)

FRONT

GRAY
SQUIRREL

3"
(7.5 CM)

REAR

Hot on the Trail

Tracks — the footprints animals make as they move — can tell you a lot about who passed through and how fast they were traveling. If the tracks are far apart, maybe the animal was running. (Picture a deer with its long strides and graceful leaps.) Do you see big and little tracks? Maybe it is the adult and its young! Look for prints in the mud or snow and check out your tracks, too — with and without your shoes!

Follow any tracks you come across and see if you can piece together something about that animal's habitat. Do the tracks end at a tree or log? Aha! Maybe you are near the animal's burrow. Or maybe the tracks end at the garbage can. Uh-oh! What does that tell you?

2"
(5 CM)

FRONT

3 1/2"
(8.5 CM)

RABBIT

REAR

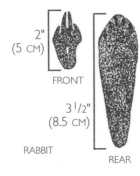

DOG

SIZE VARIES
WITH BREED

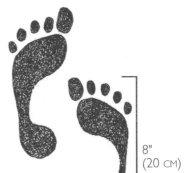

4"
(10 CM)

DEER

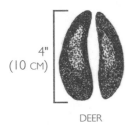

1 1/2"
(3.5 CM)

CAT

NINE-YEAR-OLD

8"
(20 CM)

Make a Wildlife Footprint Cast

Found a paw print or wildlife track in the mud that's really cool? Preserve it in plaster!

WHAT YOU NEED

Cereal-box cardboard, cut in collar shape
Tape
Large, clean can (a coffee can works well)
Measuring cup
Plaster of paris (from a hardware store)
Container of water
Large spoon
Garden trowel (or other small digging tool)
Old toothbrush

WHAT YOU DO

1. Bend the cardboard collar around the paw print or track. Fasten the ends with tape.
2. In the can, mix 1 1/2 parts plaster with 1 part water. Stir. The final consistency should be like gravy or pancake batter. Do the mixing quickly (plaster hardens in no time).
3. Pour the plaster over the print, making sure it fills the print completely. (A little overflow is OK.) Wait 30 minutes.
4. When the plaster has hardened, carefully dig around the cast and remove it from the ground. Clean off the cast, using water and the toothbrush.

Note: Please don't pour any leftover plaster down the toilet or rinse out your can in the sink. Plaster will clog the pipes!

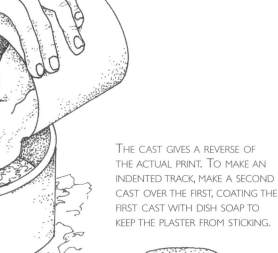

THE CAST GIVES A REVERSE OF THE ACTUAL PRINT. TO MAKE AN INDENTED TRACK, MAKE A SECOND CAST OVER THE FIRST, COATING THE FIRST CAST WITH DISH SOAP TO KEEP THE PLASTER FROM STICKING.

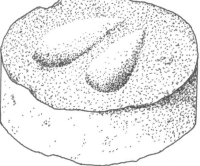

June 1 to July 1

MARK OFF FOUR STRAIGHT LINES, THEN MAKE A
DIAGONAL LINE FOR THE FIFTH SIGHTING.

Take a Wildlife Count!

Record the animals that share your habitat by making a list of all the critters you see or hear in your neighborhood. Have a contest in your family to see who can spot the most!

To record the wildlife you see, draw a symbol for each animal on a piece of poster board and tape it to your fridge or kitchen wall. Mark the dates you begin (and end) your count. Each time someone sees an animal or evidence of it, make a single vertical line next to its symbol, and note the date in the right-hand column. Once you have four lines in a row, make a crosswise mark for the fifth sighting. Continue counting by ones and fives until the end of the count.

Which animals do you see on a daily basis, and which do you spot now and then? Watch for animals at different times of day. Think of the different seasons of the year, too — what lives where you are in spring and summer? How do you think that might change in fall or winter?

Wow! Are you surprised by the number of "neighbors" you have?

Wildlife Counts That Count!

Each spring and fall, one of the most amazing mysteries of nature occurs: animal migration. Many animals move to different habitats during their life cycles to raise their young, find more plentiful food sources, or to escape harsh weather. As birds fly south in the fall or return north in the spring, they might be flying right over your house or even stopping in your yard to rest and have a snack. Or your neighborhood might be their final destination! Other animals — from clouds of insects to herds of mammals — also migrate to search for seasonal shelter and food or breeding grounds. Even earthworms are on the move!

Sad to say, human activity can affect or disrupt migration routes, some of which are hundreds of years old. That makes it all the more important to study these routes and how changes to them affect the health and well-being of animals. Join in this important effort by participating in Journey North (see Resources, page 122)! Work with other kids across North America to track the migration patterns of butterflies, birds, and mammals, and other natural events. You can also join in other national animal counts (see Resources, pages 122 to 123).

Making a Difference

Animals on the Move!

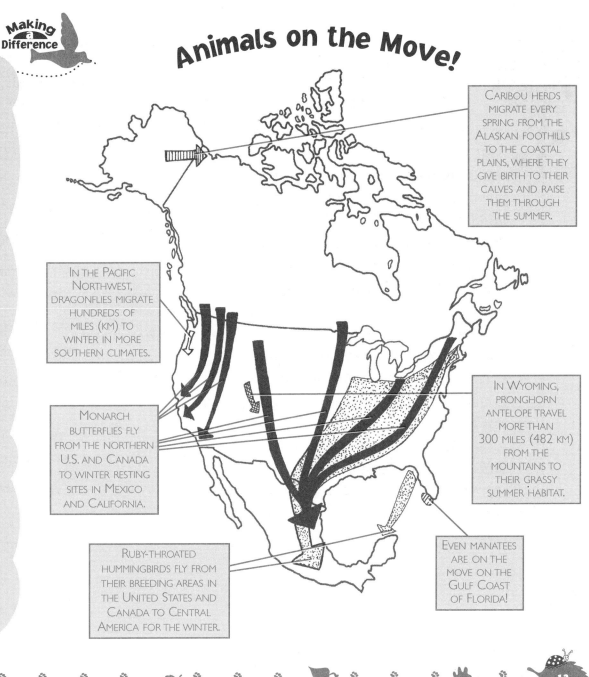

CARIBOU HERDS MIGRATE EVERY SPRING FROM THE ALASKAN FOOTHILLS TO THE COASTAL PLAINS, WHERE THEY GIVE BIRTH TO THEIR CALVES AND RAISE THEM THROUGH THE SUMMER.

IN THE PACIFIC NORTHWEST, DRAGONFLIES MIGRATE HUNDREDS OF MILES (KM) TO WINTER IN MORE SOUTHERN CLIMATES.

IN WYOMING, PRONGHORN ANTELOPE TRAVEL MORE THAN 300 MILES (482 KM) FROM THE MOUNTAINS TO THEIR GRASSY SUMMER HABITAT.

MONARCH BUTTERFLIES FLY FROM THE NORTHERN U.S. AND CANADA TO WINTER RESTING SITES IN MEXICO AND CALIFORNIA.

RUBY-THROATED HUMMINGBIRDS FLY FROM THEIR BREEDING AREAS IN THE UNITED STATES AND CANADA TO CENTRAL AMERICA FOR THE WINTER.

EVEN MANATEES ARE ON THE MOVE ON THE GULF COAST OF FLORIDA!

Take a Closer Look

Visit a "wild" spot

Now that you've discovered who lives near you, go to a nearby meadow, woods, marshy area, park, or other green, critter-friendly spot to watch and listen for what lives there. Write down every creature you observe or see evidence of. Look for animal tracks, listen for bird calls and other animal sounds, and check high and low, using your nature detective skills (SEE I SPY, page 7). Are there plants or animals you see here that you don't see at your home? If so, what is different about this habitat?

As you observe, look for different animal groups (see ANIMAL DIFFERENCES, page 15). How many of each can you identify?

The Call of the Wild

Many animals have a well-known call or sound. Whippoorwills, bobwhites, phoebes, and chickadees sing their names, for example. How many of these can you identify? And how many do you hear in your neck of the woods?

- ⊙ a melancholy cooing sound

- ⊙ steady "honk honk" high in the sky

- ⊙ series of short barks and yelps, followed by a long howl and ending with short, sharp yaps

- ⊙ steady high-pitched buzz or rattle, especially on a hot summer day

- ⊙ drawn-out trill and chatter of notes and "chuck" sounds

- ⊙ "peep, peep, peep" trilling sound near watery spots in spring

- ⊙ "Who cooks for you? Who cooks for you all?"

- ⊙ steady chirp, sounds almost like "beep beep beep"

Answers:
mourning dove; migrating ducks and geese; coyote; cicada (mating call); red squirrel; spring peepers (tiny tree frogs); barred owl; field cricket

Animal Differences

Animal Group	Natural Habitat	Characteristics	Common Examples
Fish	oceans, lakes, rivers, streams, ponds	Live in water, breathe through gills rather than lungs, have a scaly body, and move using fins.	bass, bluefish, cod, herring, perch, salmon, trout, tuna, goldfish, tropical fish
Insects	many different habitats all over the world, from deserts, caves, and fields to woods, tropical forests, lakes, and rivers	Adults have six legs; skeleton forms a hard exterior armor. Several stages of growth before adult form; **caterpillars** and **grubs** are the *larval* stage.	flies and mosquitoes; dragonflies, moths, and butterflies; beetles, termites, and ants; bees and wasps; and *many* more!
Arachnids	fields, forests, deserts, tropics	Hard outer shell; not insects because they have four pairs of legs; babies hatch from eggs and look like tiny versions of the adults.	spiders, tarantulas (different group of spiders), mites, ticks, scorpions, daddy longlegs
Amphibians	hatch from eggs laid in or near water; develop into tadpoles; grow legs and spend their adult lives on land near water (ponds, marshes, swamps)	Have a backbone but no hair, feathers, fur, or scales; breathe through their moist skin as well as their lungs. Cold-blooded (see Reptiles, below).	frogs, toads, salamanders
Reptiles	forests, deserts, tropics, near or in fresh- or salt water	Dry, scaly skin. Lay their eggs on land. *Cold-blooded:* Their bodies change temperature with the outside air.	lizards, snakes, turtles, tortoises, alligators, crocodiles
Birds	forests, fields, deserts, coastal areas, tropics, polar regions	The only animals with feathers; most birds can fly and can keep their bodies warm, and have an inner skeleton.	songbirds, woodpeckers, hawks, owls, pelicans, seagulls, ducks, geese
Mammals	forests, fields, deserts, coastal areas, tropics, polar regions, fresh and saltwater regions	Have fur or hair, can keep themselves warm, and the moms give birth to babies and feed them milk.	chipmunks, squirrels, rabbits, moles, porcupines, bats, otters, beavers, skunks — and you too!

Nature's Balancing Act

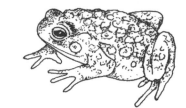

In a wildlife habitat, there has to be the right amount of food, shelter, water, and space for everyone. (Think of it like a seesaw.) You might not realize it but this balancing act is going on all around you — whether you live in the city, the suburbs, or the country! But what happens when this balance of nature is upset?

Habitat: It's Critical!

Unfortunately, every time a new housing development goes in or a shopping center is built, some animals are squeezed out of their natural habitats. Or animal habitats can be made *un*-critter-friendly by air or water pollution.

Some types of habitats — called *critical habitats* — are so important that wildlife just can't survive without them! Nesting areas for herons and other birds, water retreats for frogs and toads (egg laying sites), large wooded wintering areas where deer can *browse* (feed on plants), and milkweed plants for the monarch butterfly to feed on and raise its young are perfect examples.

THE GREAT BLUE HERON BUILDS A LARGE NEST OF STICKS IN TREETOPS IN MARSHY AREAS.

Habitat UN-Happiness

You appreciate having clean water to drink. So do your animal friends. What happens when humans pollute their water sources? Try this to find out.

Fill a 5-gallon (18.5 L) bucket with water. Sprinkle in some dirt, twigs, and pebbles. Drop in a label or piece of plastic wrap, soft-drink six-pack rings, soda pop-tops, or other typical garbage that humans throw away. Dribble a little olive oil (some of the oil from all of our cars ends up in our soil and water) and food coloring (for other forms of pollution) into the water. Stir it all up with a stick. Yuck! Imagine drinking, swimming, or laying your eggs in this water.

Now, use a strainer, cheesecloth, slotted spoon, tongs, or whatever else you can think of take the "pollution" out of the water.

How did you do? Were you able to remove most of the pollution? Some of it? Do you think you could ever get the water as clean as it was before you polluted it?

Take a Closer Look

Think about your neighborhood

Where is the closest place near your house for wild animals to live, now that humans have moved in and built homes and paved roads? What wild food is available now? What do you think happens to animals that can no longer get clean water nearby? Hmmm. If we want wildlife around to enjoy, it's up to us to preserve their habitats. And you can help!

Habitat Questions ... With Answers!

How do I attract critters to my home when I live in an apartment in the city? My yard is the playground, and my garden is a window box and some pots on the balcony.

You say a balcony is all you have? Perfect! You see, a kid's wildlife habitat doesn't have to be big to make a difference. A balcony or deck is an oasis of greenery that's especially welcomed by birds, butterflies, bees, and other small critters who find little to eat or drink among the concrete buildings, roads, and rooftops in an urban environment. A small outdoor planter filled with flowers or fruiting shrubs can be a stopover for migrating birds and butterflies. A hummingbird feeder outside your window provides an energy boost for these tiny birds who need to feed frequently.

Welcome wildlife!

Now do you see why your critter-friendly living space is so important? By creating a wildlife habitat in your yard, in a window box, or on your deck, you advertise, "Wildlife welcome here!" and help to restore some of nature's balance.

Check out pages 19 to 32 for ideas on how to get started, and use this key to help you pick activities for your outdoor space:

 Pots and smaller spots: container gardens, window boxes, building stoops and porches, decks, safe balconies, sidewalk cracks, around-a-tree habitats, alleyways, courtyards

 Larger yards or suburban areas, school sites, open spaces, fencerows

No matter what the size of the space, your wildlife habitat will make a difference. And here's the bonus: You'll have the enjoyment of watching lots of cool critters, making your outdoor space a more awesome place to hang out!

Habitat Basics

Food, water, shelter, space to roam around — those are basics needs of any animal, and what the ideal habitat provides. Let's see, you have a house or apartment where you're protected from the weather, as well as healthy food and clean water so you keep growing. And you have outdoor space like a backyard or nearby park where you can run and play in the fresh air. That sounds like a pretty nice habitat, doesn't it? Lucky you!

You can create equally special habitats that will encourage lots of different wild animals — from colorful butterflies and songbirds to turtles and chipmunks, maybe even a lizard or salamander — to be regular visitors. With just a little help from friends like you, wildlife will be quite content! Besides having lots of fun watching them, you'll play an important part in helping the wild critters that share your outdoor home.

Taking Stock

You're probably offering some of the basics
to the wildlife around you already
(think of your wildlife count, page 12).
Let's figure out exactly what you've got.
Once you figure out what's encouraging
the critters in your neighborhood
to visit or you see what's missing,
you'll know what to add. So it's time to
look around again — you know,
not just a glance but thoughtful observations
(you're getting to be a pro at that!)
while remembering the basics that
keep animals healthy and happy.

TASTY CLOVER (AND EVEN SOME DANDELIONS!) IN YOUR LAWN MIGHT ENTICE RABBITS, SHORT-TAILED SHREWS, AND WHITE-FOOTED MICE TO STICK AROUND.

EVEN PRICKLY NETTLES PROVIDE FOOD AND SHELTER FOR CRITTERS.

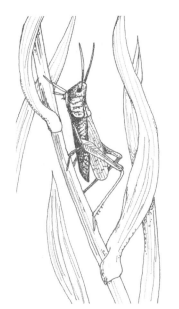

WILD GRASSY AREAS HOUSE GRASSHOPPERS AND OTHER SMALL CRITTERS.

RABBITS AND MICE LIKE TO RAISE THEIR BABIES IN BRUSH OR MULCH PILES. BE CAREFUL NOT TO DISTURB THEM IN SPRING!

A MOSSY HABITAT IS A COMFORTABLE SPOT FOR TOADS, SALAMANDERS, AND OTHER MOISTURE-LOVING ANIMALS.

"Bushes?" "Check!"

Use a handy checklist like this one to explore your outdoor space. Look everywhere — along the sides of buildings and even in the sidewalk cracks (you never know what might sprout there!). Don't overlook bushes close to your house or apartment building, window boxes, or plants in pots. Include small weedy or leafy areas on the ground — to insects, they can be a safe haven. Make a note of any spots especially suited to a specific critter.

Note: Please make your own list on a separate sheet of paper. Do not write in this book. Thank you!

Provides:	nesting spots/ nesting material	hiding spot from predators	protection from weather	food	drinking water	spot to cool off or warm up	comments
trees	✓	✓	✓				
bushes	✓	✓					
flowers				✓			
plants with berries seeds, or nuts				✓			good spot for spider web; lots of insects nearby
large or flat rocks, rock walls		✓				✓	
water source					✓		
grassy area	✓	✓					
shady area with cool, moist soil		✓				✓	lots of low-growing leafy plants perfect hiding spot for a toad!
dead standing trees	✓	✓	✓	✓			
piles of brush or leaves	✓	✓	✓	✓			
weedy areas	✓	✓		✓			

Offer It and They Will Come!

Now that you know what you have, you're ready to add to it bit by bit. (Feel as if your checklist was pretty short? That's OK! You'll see how easy it is to make some quick improvements!) Your efforts can be as simple as putting out a log for insects to hide under or hanging a feeder that will let you watch critters from your window.

Not sure what to do first? Here are some quick ideas to jump-start your wildlife habitat adventures!

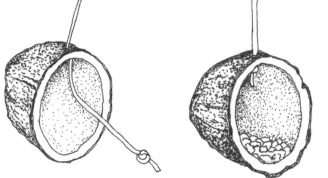

Use coconut halves as instant feeders.

Slather pinecones with peanut butter and birdseed to make a great bird snack.

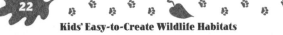

Serve up a wildlife snack bar! Encourage birds, butterflies, and other wild critters to stop by your yard by offering wildlife-friendly "fast food." String day-old bread, peanuts (in the shell), popped popcorn, orange slices, and cranberries on yarn or heavy thread. Smear pinecones with peanut butter and roll in birdseed; slather stale bread with peanut butter and jelly! For lots more feeding suggestions, see pages 33 to 66.

Offer a refreshing watering hole!

A small bath or sipping spot will attract drinkers and bathers, especially during a dry spell or when there's a deep freeze. Be creative! For more suggestions for sipping and dipping fun, see pages 99 to 120.

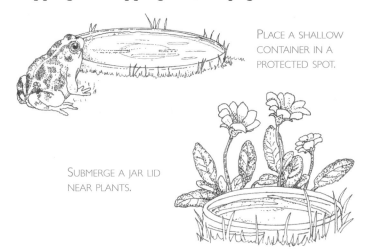

PLACE A SHALLOW CONTAINER IN A PROTECTED SPOT.

SUBMERGE A JAR LID NEAR PLANTS.

Construct an on-the-rocks sunning spot! If you

thought basking in the sun was just for beachgoers, think again! Snakes, lizards, butterflies, and dragonflies like sunning, too. A warm rock is like a welcome mat for these critters!

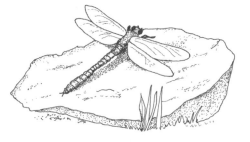

SECURE A BAKING PAN TO A BALCONY RAILING FOR AN INSTANT WATERING HOLE.

Create a wildlife mini-motel! Make a circle of logs or just set two, side by side, in a quiet sheltered spot. Sprinkle some bark mulch around for your insect friends. Presto! You've provided a home for lots of small critters. And now you've got a great spot to sit and observe! Don't forget to bring along your wildlife scrapbook (page 29).

Do Another Count!

After these wildlife welcome signs have hung out for a while, take another wildlife count (page 12). See how wildlife is finding your yard an inviting spot?

If you're inspired by what you see, you can try even more habitat ideas for food (pages 33 to 66), shelter (pages 67 to 98), and water (pages 99 to 120). And you can feel great knowing you're covering the habitat basics (see how easy it was?).

Habitat Basics

Habitat Questions ... With Answers!

Isn't creating a habitat expensive with all sorts of special plants that you have to buy? I don't have extra money to buy plants or supplies.

Not at all! As you've seen from OFFER IT AND THEY WILL COME! (page 23), a wildlife habitat certainly doesn't need to be expensive. Check out some of the other quick and easy ideas in this book, such as the wildlife brush shelter (pages 92 to 93), the rock pile (page 94), and the bee nesting block (page 76). They also use supplies that you probably already have at home.

One of the most important parts of creating a habitat is that you learn to use what you have on hand, then add to it as little or as much as you want to.

Are there trees in your yard? Or bushes that provide some protection? That's a great start. You might find that you already have some bee- or butterfly-friendly plants (page 47) in your yard; adding a water source and a landing spot will encourage more insects to come. Try making some inexpensive feeders (page 36). You can make most everything you'll use out of recycled materials. Your wildlife habitat is a "work in progress"; add to it as you feel inspired!

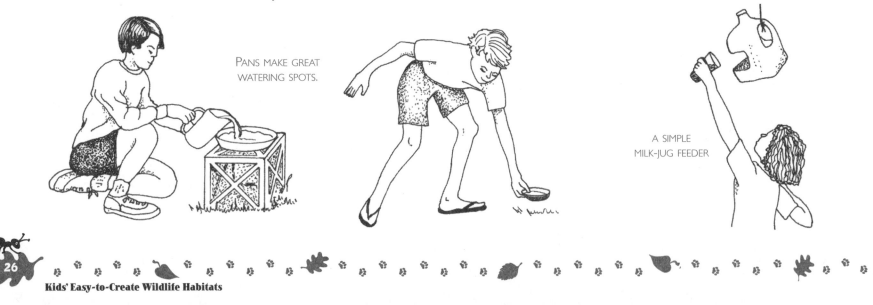

PANS MAKE GREAT WATERING SPOTS.

A SIMPLE MILK-JUG FEEDER

No Time Like the Present!

When's the best time to create a wildlife habitat? Right now! You can begin any time of year. The important thing is to get going! Many animal babies are born in early spring, so they'll need food, shelter, and safe places to hide and grow. Spring and summer are perfect times to grow wildlife-friendly plants or create a mini-garden in a pot or corner of a yard to encourage wildlife to settle in or stop by on their migration trek. During the colder months, animals wintering in northern areas will be looking extra hard for food, while those who head south will be arriving for their winter's stay. So plan ahead now to make your habitat welcoming whenever critters need an extra boost from friends like you.

Guess This Critter!

Here's a fun way to test how carefully you and your friends have been observing the wildlife around you! All you need are a few friends and a pile of pebbles. Choose someone to think of a backyard animal or insect. He or she gives a one-sentence description of his creature, such as "I'm thinking of an animal that has fur and scurries about on the ground." A player might guess "a squirrel." If she's correct, she gets a pebble. If she's wrong, she's out, and the person gives another clue. "It stuffs its cheeks with food." The person who guesses "a chipmunk" would get a pebble. Then it's someone else's turn to give clues. Whoever has the most pebbles at the end is the winner!

Kids to the Rescue!

Rx for trees, please!

Is there a tree in your yard, on the way to school, or in the park that you think is special or could use some attention? From their leafy tops to their deep-reaching roots, trees play a very important role in attracting wildlife, and in the overall environment here on planet Earth.

Like all living creatures, trees need air, water, and food. If your trees could talk, they might very well be shouting, "Feed me! Water me! Tend me!" That's especially true of trees planted along sidewalks and curbs. If their roots are covered in concrete, the soil they're growing in lacks nutrients, or they don't get enough rainwater, trees will die. You can make all the difference in a tree's life!

Here's how to help: Begin by clearing out any litter around the base of the tree. Then sprinkle natural materials like crumbled leaves, grass clippings, compost, or mulch around the base. Water trees, especially in the fall, when they often die of thirst. They need about 6 gallons (22 L) of water twice a week.

Be proud of the care you've given your tree. Sit in its shade and read *The Great Kapok Tree* by Lynne Cherry. And on Arbor Day (celebrated around April 22nd, depending on your state), team up with your family or friends to plant another tree to care for in your yard, at school, or at a local park!

Start a Wildlife Scrapbook!

What better way to show off your wildlife sightings and other habitat adventures than with a scrapbook! Use it to jot down what you observe, keep a list of the critters you see, and brainstorm ideas for improving your habitats. It's also the perfect spot for sketches or photos of your one-of-a-kind wildlife preserve through the changing seasons, and for storing special finds you've collected, like interesting seeds, pressed flowers or weeds, leaf rubbings, nuts, and seedheads. *You* decide what goes in it!

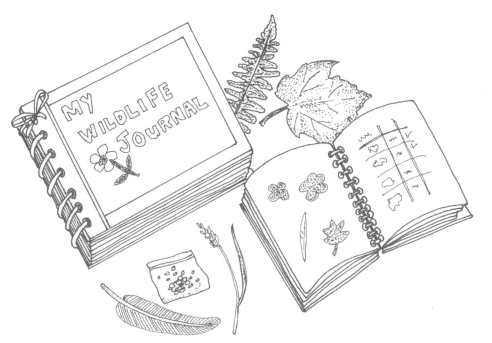

WHAT YOU NEED

For the cover: 2 sheets of stiff paper, hole punch, brass fasteners, yarn or shoelace

Cover decorations: stickers, markers, tempera paints, paintbrushes, animal illustrations from old magazines, dried flowers and leaves

Glue

White paper (for the scrapbook pages)

Clear plastic photo sleeves

Zip-locking plastic bags (for storing small items)

WHAT YOU DO

1. Decorate one sheet of stiff paper for the front cover. For fun, add paw prints to the front or as a border!

2. Place the white paper between the two covers, punch holes, and insert brass fasteners or tie it together with the yarn or shoelace.

3. Open up your scrapbook to the first page, and start dreaming, drawing, and recording your habitat adventures!

Home, Sweet Community Habitat: Kids Get Involved!

What about starting a wildlife habitat at your school, community center, church or synagogue? Neglected city parks or lots, retirement homes or senior centers, housing developments — even a flat, city building rooftop — are all possible sites! All over the country, kids are teaming up to transform their schoolyards and other community places into wildlife-friendly green spots and outdoor spaces. You and your friends can, too!

Once you've located a possible site, you'll need permission from the owner to use it. Develop a plan of what you'd like to do, the time involved, and any costs. Ask your parents, neighbors, and teachers to help you. You might find local nurseries, garden clubs, or discount stores are willing to contribute plants and supplies. Your school can even be certified as an official Schoolyard Habitat by the National Wildlife Federation! See Resources, page 121, for more information.

Making a Difference

The More, the Merrier!

The more people you have involved, the better your chances of getting permission and the more you can accomplish. Put up fliers and recruit the whole neighborhood in your habitat effort. Don't forget neighbors who don't have kids at home — they might jump at the chance to lend a hand with a project like this. Seniors often have lots of gardening know-how as well as years of volunteer experience, so tap into that great resource, too!

Your New Pets ... NOT!

OK, here's an important thing to remember as you're making all these wildlife sightings: The animals you will be welcoming are *wild* — and they should *stay wild*. Wild animals are not pets, and they won't make good pets, no matter how cute they look.

Unlike your dog or cat, which has been bred over centuries to live alongside its human friends, wild critters are best suited for living in the wild. Sadly, most wild animals will die if captured and taken home. I know you wouldn't want that to happen! Wild animals need special food and care, and they can be unpredictable, destructive, and downright dangerous when they are removed from their proper habitats. What's more, treating them as pets can turn them into pests, which leads to more problems (page 66).

Besides, while owning a pet is fun, what is so special about a wildlife habitat is its very wildness. The animals and critters in it are free to come and go as they please. If they visit or live there, it is because they want to, not because they are forced to. That's precisely what makes creating a wildlife habitat so exciting and interesting — you never quite know what you'll see from day to day.

Cute But Not Safe!

Wild mammals, such as raccoons or foxes, might carry diseases, particularly rabies, so you should NEVER touch, pet, or pick them up. That's one reason why in many areas it is against the law to capture wild animals and raise them as pets. So leave those critters to live in the wild, where they were meant to be. And if you see a wild animal acting "sick" or behaving strangely, stay far away and tell an adult immediately.

Do Not Touch!

Habitat Questions ... With Answers!

Well, why bother with a wildlife habitat if you can't touch the animals and if they might bite you?

I can see why you might think that way — especially if caring for wildlife from afar is a new idea for you. But remember, you can observe the critters, you can make a difference in a living thing's life, and if you follow the rule about not touching or getting too close, there is *very* little chance you will ever get bitten.

Plus, admit it: Some critters are lots of fun to watch, but are there any animals you really don't like, like snakes or spiders? Or maybe the moles that tunnel where you play ball? You might have more respect for them if you see the important role they play in nature. (Snakes help keep your yard and house free of rodents; moles aerate the soil with their tunneling; spiders catch insects and flies.)

Learn to appreciate how each type of wildlife has its own way of gathering food, finding shelter, and raising its young. Take time out of each day to enjoy wildlife — whether it's watching a pigeon pecking, a chipmunk scurrying, a bee buzzing, or a bat swooping. Having wild critters around reminds us that we share the earth with *all* its creatures. Keeping them healthy and happy in *their* habitat is important to *our* habitat's health and happiness, too!

Come & Get It!

Fast Food for Animal Friends

When you pack a lunch or want a snack with your friends after school, what do you do? Chances are, you check the cupboard and refrigerator for yummy foods (and healthy ones, I hope! OK, a cookie or two is allowed, too). Well, animals need plenty of nutritious foods, just like you. And their "cupboards" are the flowers, trees, plants, berries, seeds, and insects they find in the wild. Insects, in turn, search for food on plants and in the soil. So if you want your critter friends to stop by and stick around for a while, do what any good host would do — serve them some of those same snacks right in your yard!

Calling All Birds!

Offering your feathered friends some tasty treats will attract them to your wildlife habitat in a hurry, and it's one of the easiest ways to advertise your space as a wildlife-friendly place. In fact, you're likely to see chipmunks, squirrels, and other small critters stopping by for a snack as well.

Bird Fare Basics

Are there some foods you love to eat anytime (candy might be one, I'll bet!) and others (maybe brussels sprouts or lima beans) that you don't mind skipping altogether? Well, your feathered friends are a lot like you: They have foods they like more than others. Seed-eating birds, like chickadees and finches, prefer sunflower and thistle seed, while others (woodpeckers and wrens) will munch on insects if given a chance. Still others (orioles, tanagers, and hummingbirds, for example) sip nectar or eat fruit. And of course, there are also some "piggish birds" — starlings, for one — who will eat just about anything you put out. The trick is to keep them from hogging the feast!

Birds can be picky about *where* they eat, too. Some prefer hanging feeders, others like to eat from a platform or tray, and still others prefer their seed sprinkled on the ground.

So what's a bird-lover like you to do? Offer a variety of favorite foods (page 38) in different types of feeders as shown in this section so you're sure to attract whoever is flying by!

Feeder Frenzy

You've probably seen all sorts of feeders at garden centers or hardware stores, and you might be, well, *expensive* (especially for a kid on an allowance!). I've got some good news for you: Feeders don't have to be complicated and costly — in fact, simpler is usually better!

To create a smorgasbord the birds can't resist, start off with a few of the homemade hanging feeders shown here as well a platform feeder (page 41), filled with the bird-food favorites on page 38. Then stand back and watch the action!

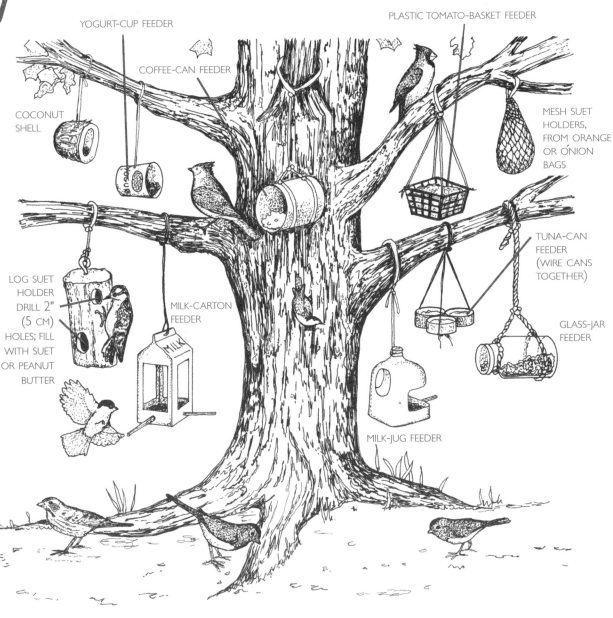

YOGURT-CUP FEEDER

PLASTIC TOMATO-BASKET FEEDER

COFFEE-CAN FEEDER

COCONUT SHELL

MESH SUET HOLDERS, FROM ORANGE OR ONION BAGS

LOG SUET HOLDER DRILL 2" (5 CM) HOLES; FILL WITH SUET OR PEANUT BUTTER

MILK-CARTON FEEDER

TUNA-CAN FEEDER (WIRE CANS TOGETHER)

GLASS-JAR FEEDER

MILK-JUG FEEDER

WILDLIFE WREATH

Decorate a vine wreath with corncobs, sunflowers, fruit slices, cranberries, chokecherries, nuts, and other natural bird and wildlife foods.

Take a Closer Look

Be a backyard birder!

While the birds are feasting away, you'll be able to observe them up close from a window without scaring them away. Some birds you may recognize right away, others may be unfamiliar. Interested in identifying the birds at your feeders? Two very handy tools are a pair of binoculars and a field guide (see Resources, page 122). Listen for songs and calls, too. The whippoorwill, bobwhite, phoebe, and chickadee are all named for their sounds.

Bird-Food Favorites

Black-oil sunflower seed: Just getting started feeding the birds? Serve up some black-oil sunflower seed! It's the hands-down favorite! These small, black seeds have a thin shell that's easy to crack. The larger, striped sunflower seeds are difficult for small birds to eat. For even more fun, try growing your own sunflowers (pages 44 to 45).

Suet: Just another name for white beef fat. Great source of energy for birds that live in cold-winter climates, like nuthatches, chickadees, and woodpeckers.

Peanuts: Serve the unroasted and unsalted type (in the shell).

Cracked corn: Sparrows, finches, blackbirds, doves, quails, and squirrels all say YUM!

Safflower seed: A cardinal favorite; chickadees, finches, grosbeaks, nuthatches, and doves like it too.

Millet: Most birds like the white millet better than the red. Ground-feeders such as juncos, doves, and sparrows like it.

Niger/thistle seed: For finches and other small birds.

Fruit: Grapes (and grape jelly!), sliced citrus fruits, apples, bananas, and even melons will attract robins, tanagers, orioles, titmice, and mockingbirds.

Collect Wild Food

Team up with Mother Nature to feed the birds! In late summer and fall, look for ripe berries and wildflower seeds to harvest for serving up at your feeders. Go with an adult so you can be sure what's safe to pick, and get permission first if you are foraging on someone else's property. Harvest only the fruit, leaving the plants in place to provide more food for wildlife. Wild blueberries, raspberries, blackberries, and grapes are all popular bird fare, for example. Here are some other bird-pleasing foods you might find.

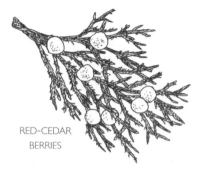

RED-CEDAR BERRIES

JUNIPER BERRIES

BLACK-EYED SUSANS WITHOUT THE PETALS LOOK LIKE FUZZY BROWN GUMDROPS STUCK ON THE ENDS OF STICKS!

HAWS FROM HAWTHORNS

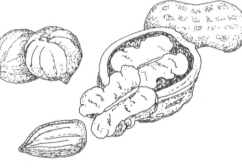

COLLECT DIFFERENT KINDS OF NUTS, AND CRACK OPEN THOSE WITH A HARD SHELL (LIKE WALNUTS AND HICKORIES) BEFORE SERVING.

THISTLE SEED IS A FAVORITE FOOD OF SMALL BIRDS.

SERVICEBERRIES

CHOKECHERRIES

39

Come & Get It! Fast Food for Animal Friends

Handy Hummer Feeder

Hummingbirds beat their wings an incredible 70 times per second, enabling them to fly forward and backward, and even to hover in one spot. All that beating sure takes a lot of energy … and that's where your feeders really help! Fill this easy-to-make hummer feeder with sugar water.

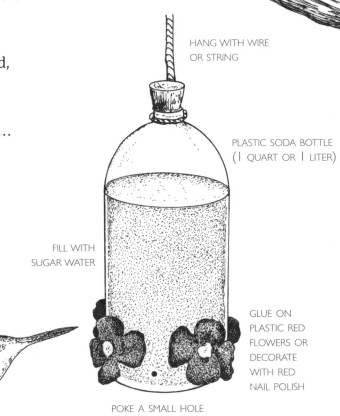

HANG WITH WIRE OR STRING

PLASTIC SODA BOTTLE (1 QUART OR 1 LITER)

FILL WITH SUGAR WATER

GLUE ON PLASTIC RED FLOWERS OR DECORATE WITH RED NAIL POLISH

POKE A SMALL HOLE

Sugar water: A humdinger of a hummingbird food (and a favorite of bees and butterflies, too!). To make, heat $1/4$ cup (50 ml) sugar (*not* honey) and $1/4$ cup (50 ml) water in a heavy saucepan until the mixture comes to a boil. Remove from the stove and stir in $3/4$ cup (175 ml) cold water. Cool completely before filling feeder. The sugar water may be stored up to a week in the refrigerator.

Take-It-Easy Tray Feeder

Serve berries, other fruits, and seeds, in style for your platform-feeding feathered friends. Only put out enough food for a day or two.

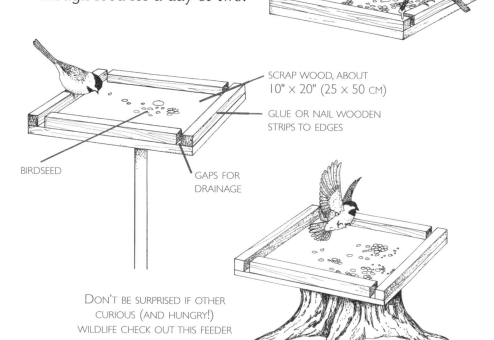

SCRAP WOOD, ABOUT
10" × 20" (25 × 50 CM)

GLUE OR NAIL WOODEN
STRIPS TO EDGES

BIRDSEED

GAPS FOR
DRAINAGE

DON'T BE SURPRISED IF OTHER
CURIOUS (AND HUNGRY!)
WILDLIFE CHECK OUT THIS FEEDER

Habitat Questions ... With Answers!

I'm afraid my cat will catch the birds and chipmunks that visit my feeders. What can I do to help keep the wildlife safe?

I can't deny the facts: Cats, both strays and favorite pets, are definitely bad news for the songbirds, chipmunks and other small mammals, and toads that visit your habitat. The best thing to do is to keep cats inside, as indoor pets. If you're starting off with a new kitten as a pet, keep it indoors — if it has never been outside, it won't know what it's missing, and the wild critters will be safer. (Your kitten will be safer indoors, too!)

To guard your wildlife visitors from the outdoor neighborhood cats, offer wildlife cover by building a small brush pile (pages 92 to 93) or offering some shrubbery for them to hide in. Keep your feeders about 10' (3 m) away from the cover, so wild animals can make an easy escape without being ambushed by crouching cats lying in wait.

Restaurant Rules: Keep it Clean!

One very important rule to keep birds and other critters coming to feast is to keep your food feeders clean. Birds can become sick from leftover bits of seeds and hulls that become moldy, and from bird droppings on feeder trays. Replace the food every two days or so and clean your feeders once a week (every three to four days for hummingbird feeders). Scrub the feeder with soap and water, rinse well, and let the feeder air-dry before refilling. Be sure to wash your hands after cleaning any feeder.

At least once a season, disinfect your feeders with a solution of one part bleach to nine parts water (get adult help for this, please — bleach is poisonous!).

And thanks for keeping your feathered customers healthy!

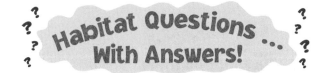

Habitat Questions ... With Answers!

OK, I like squirrels, but they keep eating all the food I put out for the birds. How can I make sure the birds get their fair share? I'm also worried I might be attracting mice and rats, which won't make my neighbors too happy.

Squirrels can be quite comical to watch, but they sure can hog the feast, can't they? One way to prevent them from raiding your feeders is to add a pie-tin baffle below the feeder. You can also try offering them their own banquet to keep them occupied (page 63).

Rats are a different problem. I can see why your neighbors might get upset! To keep rats or other unwanted rodents from congregating around your feeders, rake up any food that falls to the ground. If you are feeding the birds in a small yard or on a balcony, choose birdseed that already has the hulls removed, so there is less spilled or discarded food.

If squirrels and rodents are a continuing problem at your feeders, think about *growing* your birdseed instead (pages 44 to 45). For city spaces, hummingbird feeders (page 40) and butterfly gardens (page 55) are great alternatives that will let you enjoy some "wild" visitors without the pest problems.

CONIFER (EVERGREEN) TREES OFFER BIRDS SHELTER AND SEEDS TO EAT.

NASTURTIUMS, TRUMPET VINES, PINK PETUNIAS, AND **FUCHSIA** WELCOME HUMMINGBIRDS!

PURPLE CONEFLOWERS ARE EASY TO GROW, AND BIRDS LOVE THE BUSHY BALL-LIKE SEEDHEADS IN THE FALL.

Homegrown Harvest!

A habitat planted for birds and other critters doesn't have to be complicated or demand a lot of time and space to provide food and a sheltered snacking spot.

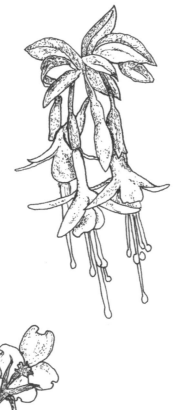

BLUEBERRY BUSHES, RASPBERRIES, AND **STRAWBERRIES** ALL GROW WELL IN POTS OR PLANTERS, AND PROVIDE YUMMY SNACKS FOR YOU AS WELL AS FOR THE BIRDS!

DOGWOODS AND **CRABAPPLES** DRAW BIRDS TO THEIR FRUIT.

Sow Serve-Yourself Sunflowers!

Plant these homegrown bird feeders along a sidewalk; in containers on a balcony, porch, or terrace; or in a small space in your yard. Sunflowers come in all colors and sizes, from reach-your-knees small to over-your-head tall, and they're one of the easiest flowers to grow. My favorite sunflower variety is the Mammoth Russian that gets up to 12' (3 m) tall. Sunflowers give you loads of big, bright bouquets all season long — and provide a self-serve feast for the birds come fall!

WHAT YOU NEED

Sunny plot of soil or container and planting mix
  (available from hardware stores or garden centers)
Garden rake
Sunflower seed packets (available from garden
  centers or grocery stores)
Trowel or hoe
Watering can

WHAT YOU DO

1. If you're planting directly in the ground, prepare the plot for planting by yanking out all weeds and loosening the top 6" (15 cm) of soil. Rake the surface smooth. If using a container, make sure it has drainage holes, then fill it about three-fourths full of planting mix.

2. Plant the seeds according to the seed packet directions. Cover with soil and pat down firmly. Keep the soil moist until the seedlings emerge.

3. Watch them grow! When the big blooms and seedheads form, feel free to cut a few for bouquets, but leave the rest for the birds. Your feathered friends will gobble them right off the plants. Or, cut the flowers and place them on the deck or other nearby spot where you can watch the birds feast up close. To save some seeds for later bird feasts, let the seedheads dry. Store the dried seeds in a jar.

Lunch Special: Insects to Go!

Encourage wrens, song sparrows, or woodpeckers, as well as other insect-loving critters such as shrews and moles, to hang around by bringing out the insect appetizers. Dead limbs, decaying logs, leafy retreats at the bases of bushes or trees, or bark mulch around bushes or on paths all offer super hideouts for adult insects and their larvae (commonly called caterpillars). For more insect-friendly shelter spots you can add to your yard, see pages 75 to 77.

Mealworms (beetle larvae) are particular favorites of insect-eaters, especially in winter when fresh food is in short supply. You can buy them at bait, garden supply, or pet stores, or see Resources, page 123.

Take a Closer Look

A sap trap!

Ever notice a line of evenly "drilled" holes in the trunk of a tree? It's probably the work of a sapsucker. These woodpeckers peck the holes and then fly off. The holes fill with sap, and when insects crawl or fly to the sweet stuff, they get stuck. When the sapsucker returns, it finds tasty insect treats, nicely sweetened! Yum!

Making a Difference

Counting the Birds

Is the arrival of a robin one of the first signs of spring where you live? Then you probably live in the northern half of the country. Or, if robins hang out all winter at your home and then head north in spring, you likely live in a more southern location. Either place, birds are flying by your window, some staying just to refuel while others camp out for the whole season. Keep track of who flies by by participating in one of the national bird counts (see Resources, page 122).

And, hey, thanks for caring enough to count! Input from wildlife watchers like you all over North America is used to track bird populations and migration routes, so the information is really important and appreciated. Way to go, kiddo!

Feasts for Butterflies and Bees

Bring your yard alive with colorful butterflies! In the process, you'll also attract the beautiful moths, hummingbirds, bees, and wasps that help *pollinate* (move pollen from flower to flower) our plants. Offer some simple shelters and nesting sites (pages 67 to 98).

Diner's Delight

Serve the butterflies in your neighborhood a buffet of sweetened fruit, and expect to see a few other bird and insect visitors as well!

WHAT YOU NEED
Sugar water (right)
Knife (use with adult help)
Ripe bananas
Strawberries
Watermelon
Apples
Shallow bowl or pie pan

WHAT YOU DO
1. Make sugar water by mixing 2 to 3 teaspoons (10 to 15 ml) of granulated sugar into about 1/2 cup (125 ml) of boiling water. Let cool.
2. Slice the fruit into the container. Add the sweetened water to the fruit. Place the dish on a porch or bench, or in the garden. Watch as butterflies and other flying friends arrive for dinner!

Take a Closer Look

Is it a butterfly or a moth?

If you see it during the day, chances are it's a butterfly. Moths are more active at night, while butterflies like the heat of the day. Watch it land: If it holds its wings up, it's a butterfly. If it rests with its wings down, it's a moth.

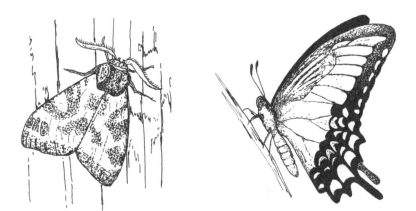

THE CATERPILLAR OF THE EASTERN BLACK SWALLOWTAIL BUTTERFLY FEEDS ON PLANTS IN THE CARROT FAMILY, INCLUDING QUEEN ANNE'S LACE, PARSLEY, AND DILL.

Butterfly Baby Food

Like many animals, butterflies eat entirely different things when they are young than when they are grown-up. Adult butterflies sip on nectar, especially from flowers with red, yellow, orange, pink, or purple blossoms. But during their larval, or caterpillar, life stage, butterflies munch on leaves, eating maybe just one or two plant types. The caterpillar of the monarch butterfly (page 50) munches only on milkweed leaves, for example. Other butterfly larvae favorites are nettles and thistles.

Ask your mom what you ate when you were a baby. How was it different from what you eat now?

Take a closer Look

Open a bug dessert bar!

Here's another great way to watch a variety of insects — they'll be so busy stuffing themselves, they'll let you get up close and personal to quietly observe them.

Mash an overripe banana with some brown sugar and let the mixture sit for a couple of hours. Slather it on the bark of a tree. Insects will come creeping, crawling, flying, you name it, as soon as they smell that sweet stuff. Recognize anyone? Insects seem to love sweet treats as much as we humans do!

Come back with a flashlight after dark. Are there more bugs? Fewer? What different kinds of insects do you notice?

The Marvelous Monarch

Chances are, you already know the beautiful orange, black, and white-spotted monarch butterfly. But did you know what a picky eater the monarch is?

Momma monarchs lay creamy white eggs on the undersides of milkweed leaves — and on nothing else! A tiny caterpillar hatches from the egg and munches on milkweed leaves, getting larger and larger until it bursts right out of its skin (four times, in fact). When large enough, the black, yellow, and white caterpillar spins itself a cocoon-like *chrysalis*, where it goes through an incredible mystery of nature called *metamorphosis* and changes into a beautiful butterfly! While most adult butterflies live for just 10 to 20 days, some monarchs live for as long as six months, traveling to the mountains of central Mexico for the winter and then back again in the spring — a distance of thousands of miles (km)!

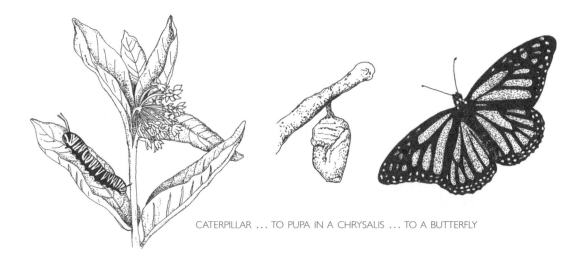

CATERPILLAR ... TO PUPA IN A CHRYSALIS ... TO A BUTTERFLY

Monarch Watch

Making a Difference

Join with other kids across the continent to map the location of monarchs and help to monitor their populations and habitats. The Monarch Watch group is devoted to helping and observing the monarch butterfly — and it could use your help! See Resources, page 122.

Kids to the Rescue!

Save the milkweed!

Remember about critical habitats (page 16)? Adult monarchs lay their eggs *only* on milkweed plants and monarch caterpillars eat *only* milkweed, so that makes the wild milkweed plant, well, critical! The problem is, when meadows are plowed up for hayfields or (even worse) bulldozed for parking lots and malls, all those milkweed plants — the monarch's habitat — are lost too.

Help to protect the monarch by making sure there's plenty of milkweed to go around. Scout out milkweed plants in construction sites and other areas that are being developed. Ask for permission to transplant them to your yard or school before the plants are mowed or trampled (pages 52 to 53). Or, gather milkweed seeds from wild plants and tend a patch of homegrown milkweed in a planter or small sunny patch of soil. If every kid — whether in the city, suburb, or rural area — grows several milkweed plants each year in safe places near homes and schools, the monarchs' milkweed habitats will survive. It's as simple as that!

save our milkweed!

Make a Milkweed "Wild" Spot

To watch butterflies in their different life stages, you need to offer a place for them to lay eggs, caterpillar food, twigs or branches to which caterpillars can secure a hanging chrysalis, and nectar sources for the hungry adults. The milkweed plant can do all those things for the monarch! (For other plants to add to a butterfly garden, see SUPER-SIMPLE BUTTERFLY & BEE BOUQUET, page 55.)

WHAT YOU NEED

A sunny garden spot or a large container with drainage holes about three-fourths full of planting mix (available from hardware stores or garden centers)
Milkweed plants
Shovel
Bucket
Watering can

WHAT YOU DO

1. In early spring or summer, prepare a planting site in a sunny spot, at the edge of your lawn or by a fence, for example, or in the container. You need a hole at least 1' (30 cm) deep.

2. With an adult, look for young green milkweed plants growing in a vacant lot or field that will be mowed or plowed under. Use the shovel to dig a large circle around the stem, being careful not to injure the roots.

3. Place the plant and a good portion of the roots and soil in the bucket. Transport it to your prepared hole or planter. Fill the hole with water, then place the milkweed plant in. Fill around the plant with soil and press firmly.

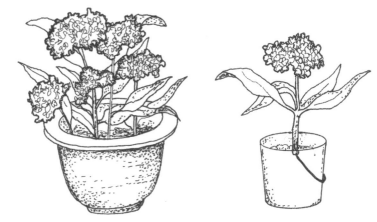

4. Water your milkweed plant every other day. In late summer and fall, watch as your milkweed makes its big seedpods filled with silky white tufts. Each tuft unfurls and acts like a tiny parachute, carrying its precious cargo along on the slightest breeze! Plant those seeds for more milkweed in the spring!

Take a Closer Look

Fuzzy bear or woolly moth?

Have you ever seen woolly bear caterpillars — those hairy brown-banded black caterpillars that come out in early fall? Some people believe that the wider the brown band, the worse the winter will be! The woolly bear lives in winter curled up beneath logs and in hollows, wrapped in a cocoon. In spring it emerges as a plain moth known as the Isabella tiger moth!

What a Butterfly Wants

If a butterfly could leave you a habitat wish list, what would be on it?

A ready supply of nectar. With the easy-to-grow flowers on page 55, you'll be all set!

A sunny spot out of the wind where adult butterflies can warm their wings. (I've seen butterflies and dragonflies resting in the warmth on the sunny side of buildings or even on a white sheet hung on the clothesline on a sunny day!) So locate butterfly plantings in a protected spot and set a flat rock nearby for a warm resting spot.

A "butterfly puddle" (a shallow container set in or near the plants and filled with water) so they can stop and sip, too.

PURPLISH COPPER

RED ADMIRAL

CLOUDED SULPHUR

Super-Simple Butterfly & Bee Bouquets

Chances are, if you have flowers outside — in hanging baskets, in planters or window boxes, or out in the yard — you are already offering some butterfly faves. Butterflies are attracted to red, orange, yellow, pink, and purple flowers, especially when planted in clumps of a single color so they can easily find them. Bees will come to most flowering plants, especially those with blue and yellow flowers. Wasps like herbs and other plants with lots of tiny flowers.

Use these easy-to-grow flowers to create butterfly retreats in a jiffy just about anywhere.

Annuals (they grow for only one season): cosmos, marigolds, petunias, zinnias

Perennials (grow from year to year): asters, bee balm, butterfly weed, daisies, daylilies, goldenrod, milkweed, purple coneflower, mint, yarrow

Make a window box resting spot of marigolds, cosmos, petunias, or zinnias for butterflies and bees.

Decorate with daylilies. Deck a deciduous tree with daylilies at its base. The flowers will make a beautiful ring around the trunk, growing thicker over time, and because you won't have to trim or mow, the tree's roots will be protected.

Plant a pot of mint. The butterflies and bees will love the flowers, and you can carefully harvest the leaves to make your own mint tea!

Pesticide **FREE!**

Kids to the Rescue!

No pesticides, please!

One of the most important things you can do to make your yard a better place for wildlife is to ask your parents and neighbors to eliminate, or at least reduce, their use of pesticides and herbicides. These chemicals kill the bees, butterflies, and other insects you are trying to welcome to your yard. And chemicals that are poisonous to plants and animals are likely to be poisonous to kids and pets, too! Just that one change will go a long way in putting out the welcome mat for bees, butterflies, frogs, toads, and other critters.

Not sure how to ask? Here's one suggestion: Go around to your neighborhood and explain that you are starting a wildlife habitat in your yard or wanting to attract more birds, bees, and butterflies (make it clear you are not going to encourage raccoons and skunks!). Ask your neighbors if they will help you by reducing the amount of pesticides or herbicides they use on their plants and yards. If everyone in your neighborhood made that one change, it could really make a difference!

More Snacks for Small Creatures

The amazing thing about starting a wildlife habitat is that once you begin feeding one critter, other animals will come out to dine, too. Toads and other amphibians, shrews, and bats will all appreciate insects that come to lunch; squirrels, mice, and chipmunks will gobble up birdseed; and rabbits will happily feast on flowering plants and a helping of garden vegetables. The trick is to cater your wildlife buffet to the needs of the animals you'd most like to attract, while keeping less-welcome guests away.

Chipmunks on Patrol!

If you feed birds in your yard, chances are you will also attract chipmunks. You can spot these cute little critters running along stone walls or visiting platform feeders on the ground. They eat a diet based on seeds and nuts, with earthworms, insects, berries, cherry and plum pits, mushrooms, and eggs on the side. To make your habitat "chipmunk friendly," leave a plastic lid filled with water beside rocks so they can drink in safety. And provide a pile of rocks (page 94), small woodpile, or brush shelter (pages 92 to 93) nearby so that they have a safe place to dash in case of danger.

Give Your Lawn a Lift!

 Most homesites, if they have any greenery at all, have most of it as lawn. It's the main event. And you gotta admit it, lawns are mighty great for doing handstands, playing ball, and running in a game of tag. So, no, I'm not saying you should dig it all up. Just give it some highlights to make it more interesting for wildlife. Think of it as "controlled wildness."

Bring on the clover and daisies. Rabbits, mice, and insects prefer a more natural lawn with some variety, and it's a lot nicer for the rest of us, too. Make a daisy chain as you skip around barefoot on the soft green grass!

Let a fence flourish. Rather than trimming and mowing around fences, let the grass grow tall and develop seedheads. Once you stop mowing, daisies, yarrow, goldenrod, and other wildflowers will have a chance to grow, too. You've just created a safe haven (with delicious seed snacks!) for insects, birds, and other small critters. *And* it's less work for you!

Start a seedling nursery. Have you ever noticed the bright green shoots that come up in your lawn, especially in spring before the first grass is mown? They're tiny tree seedlings. Some of the seedlings may even have the seed coatings still attached, like the "wings" of maple seeds. To wildlife, it's a tasty treat, and if left to grow, a mighty oak might form! Leave a patch of the grass unmown in a corner of your yard so the seedlings can feed the wildlife at ground level, along with the ferns, wildflowers, and weeds that crop up.

Come & Get It! Fast Food for Animal Friends

Predator or Prey: To Be or Not to Be ... Eaten!

Every animal — including you — has a common need to eat. No question there: That's how we get our nourishment to stay strong and healthy. What's so fascinating in Mother Nature's scheme of things is how different critters eat different foods — including other critters. What you eat and who eats you determines whether you are a hunter, or a *predator*, or the hunted, the *prey!*

Plant-eaters, or *herbivores*, like rabbits and deer, have the challenge of finding enough to eat while avoiding being caught by meat-eating hunters, or *carnivores*, like foxes, coyotes, hawks, and owls. Many animals are both predators and prey, depending on who is around. As *omnivores*, skunks and opossums (commonly called possums) eat both plants and animals, yet they are also hunted by predators like *fishers* (a member of the weasel family) and coyotes. And small predators become prey when they are hunted by larger predators!

It might seem sort of cruel at first that in order for a predator to live, a prey must die. But that's not a bad thing at all, actually. It's a connected web of life, in which some animals must eat others in order to survive, and is part of Mother Nature's amazing system. It is designed to keep animal populations in balance and ensure that there is enough food to go around — and when humans don't interfere, it works just fine!

A RABBIT MUST HIDE OR ESCAPE QUICKLY, OR IT MAY BECOME ANOTHER ANIMAL'S LUNCH!

Kids' Easy-to-Create Wildlife Habitats

Look for Owl Pellets

Owls can be found throughout North America, in all sorts of different habitats, from the cold arctic tundra to the sunny climates of Florida and the southwestern U.S. This means that there is probably an owl species that lives near you! One way to check if these winged predators are around is to look for signs that they've been eating.

Owls eat mice, rabbits, insects, and other small animals — even other birds! Because (like other birds) owls have no teeth, they swallow their prey whole, bones and all. Then, whatever they can't digest, they *regurgitate* (re-GUR-ji-tate) as oblong *pellets* of fur, feathers, and bones. It might sound a little gruesome, but these tidy little bundles are really cool to find.

Look for owl pellets at the bases of trees and other areas you might expect owls to nest in, such as barns. Dissect a pellet to find out what the bird has been eating. Using gloves, break one in half and soak it in warm water until it loosens up. Pour off the water and pick the pellet apart with a toothpick. Can you figure out what the owl might have eaten?

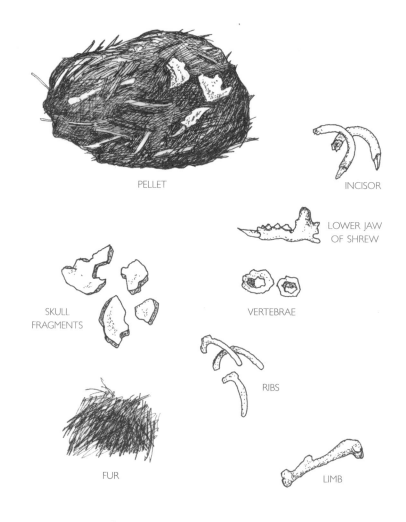

PELLET

INCISOR

LOWER JAW OF SHREW

SKULL FRAGMENTS

VERTEBRAE

RIBS

FUR

LIMB

CHECK OUT THE CONTENTS OF THIS PELLET. WHAT DID THIS OWL EAT?

Come & Get It! Fast Food for Animal Friends

Play Possum & Coyote

Try "playing possum" with a game of your own! Play this game with two or more people — the more players you have, the more fun it is. Pick one player to be the Coyote, then put on some favorite music, and have all the Possums dance around with all sorts of silly movements. The person who is the Coyote suddenly turns the music off, and the Possums must freeze into total stillness. No Possum can move a muscle, or move to a more comfortable position: You have to stay just as you were when the music stopped! The Coyote walks around trying to make one of the Possums smile, laugh, move, giggle, or blink. If a Possum moves or makes a noise, the Coyote will have caught you and you're out. The last one left in gets to be the Coyote next time.

Playing Possum

Have you ever heard the expression "playing possum"? It means keeping so still that you look dead! Possums don't really think about "pretending" to play possum, though — they just act that way naturally! It's one of their ways of trying to avoid being a predator's lunch.

A possum threatened by a predator first shows its mouthful of sharp teeth, growls, and hisses sort of like an angry cat. If that doesn't work, the possum may try to run away. But if the predator, such as a dog, coyote, or a fisher, grabs the possum, it goes limp with its eyes wide open and its tongue hanging out, just as if it were dead. Sometimes this trick works, and the predator loses interest. The possum may continue to appear dead for several hours, however, just to be on the safe side!

Outsmart the Squirrels ... With a Feast of Their Own!

If squirrels are crashing the party at the bird feeders, why not try attracting them to their own buffet instead? Set the squirrel feeder away from your other feeders so the birds can get a bite to eat. Gather acorns and other nuts for the squirrels to enjoy, too.

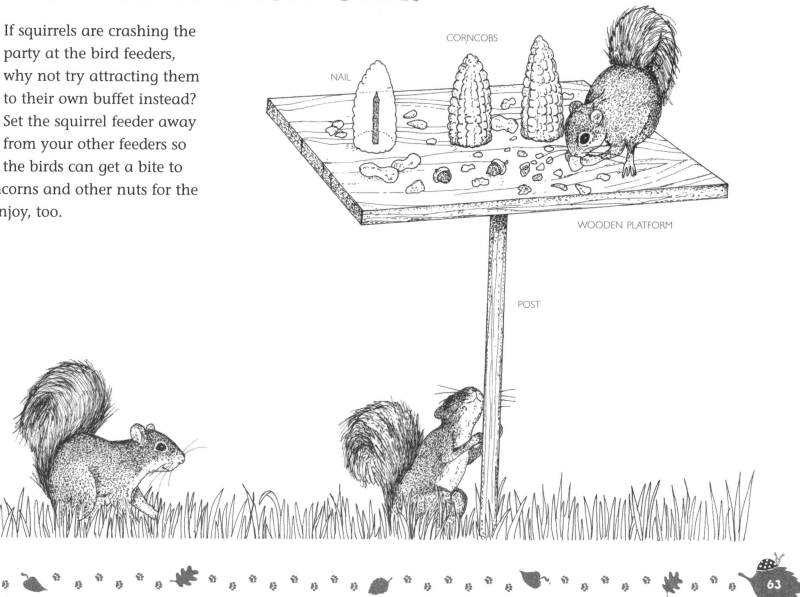

NAIL

CORNCOBS

WOODEN PLATFORM

POST

Take a Closer Look

Squirreling away

Watch squirrels gathering nuts. They seem so determined and sure about what they are doing! The truth is, squirrels don't actually remember *where* they bury every single nut — they rely on their sense of smell to find them when they need them. They can smell them even under a thick layer of snow! But sometimes they never find them at all!

What kinds of squirrels do you have around your yard? Red squirrels are smaller than the gray squirrels and not quite as noisy (though they can be a pest if they try to get in your attic to nest!). Flying squirrels don't actually have wings so they don't really fly. They have folds of loose skin under their arms. When they stretch out their arms, it pulls the skin tight. It's quite a sight to see one "sail" from one branch to another!

Nut Hunt Fun

Is your memory or sense of smell as keen as a squirrel's? Count out about 25 nuts — unshelled peanuts or other nuts work fine — and then bury or hide them in secret places indoors or out. Leave them for two days, then return and start your hunt. Try to find the nuts by memory and by using your sniffing sense, just as a squirrel does!

Look for clues, using your other senses, too. Is the soil disturbed? Does walking in a familiar spot help you remember where you hid them?

Count your finds. How successful were you? Now, imagine being a squirrel and finding all your winter's food using your sense of smell!

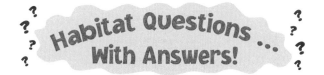

Habitat Questions ... With Answers!

I've heard that it's not a good idea to give wildlife, other than birds and butterflies, handouts of extra food, especially in the city. Is that true?

You ask a very good question! While wildlife *plantings*, like trees, flowers, shrubs, and berries are always welcome, large handouts of extra food in feeders or on the ground can sometimes cause a problem, especially in the city. While you may enjoy the commotion a few squirrels create, for example, your neighbors won't appreciate an army of squirrels emptying bird feeders, eating garden vegetables and fruits, and digging up their flower bulbs. So while it's OK to offer squirrels a snack, please don't put out bushels of seed, or you may create a problem (*and* irritate your neighbors), rather than creating a habitat that mimics nature's balance.

Some wildlife shouldn't be fed at all. Larger animals, such as deer, possums, raccoons, skunks, and bears, exist best on natural food in the wild. When fed extra handouts such as pet food or garbage scraps, these animals come too close to where humans live and they become pests, rather than animals we appreciate occasionally glimpsing. And sometimes they become dangerous as they lose their fear of humans. Feeding them causes problems for other species, such as birds, reptiles, amphibians, insects, and other smaller mammals, too!

Too Many Raccoons

A raccoon's natural habitat is along streambanks and in the woods. It eats grapes, nuts, berries, grubs, grasshoppers, crickets, voles, deer mice, squirrels and other small mammals, plus bird eggs and nestlings. But because a raccoon can eat just about anything, it can exist on human food, too, so it becomes a pest around cities and suburbs. I've seen a pair of raccoons climbing in and out of the dumpster at a restaurant in a busy section of town in broad daylight, while people walked and drove by. These hungry critters were totally unafraid of the humans around them! And that's not good for the raccoons or for people.

Kids to the Rescue!

Prevent raccoon raids

Are raccoons a problem where you live? Imagine you're a hungry raccoon and go for a walk in your neighborhood to see how many kinds of food you can find. Remember, raccoons will eat just about anything — berries, eggs, even your leftover pizza!

Ask an adult to help you clean up and make your neighborhood coon-proof! Secure trash-can lids or find other places to store the cans, and protect compost piles and gardens with fencing and even a lid if necessary. Good work! And thanks for being a habitat helper!

Simple Shelters

Home, Sweet Home for Animal Friends

Your home, whether it's many floors above a bustling city, tucked into a suburban neighborhood, or out in the country, is your sheltered spot where you're protected from cold or heat, wind and rain. Inside your safe haven, you can relax and rest with your family.

That's pretty much what wild critters want in a residence, too — someplace safe where they can hide from predators and raise their young, sheltered from bad weather. Make it easy for birds, butterflies, bats, chipmunks, and other wildlife to feel safe and protected in your yard. You don't need anything fancy! With sticks, stones, brush, flowerpots, and scrap wood, as well as nesting materials, you can make artful abodes and cozy homes to suit all kinds of animal friends. You can even make an awesome observatory for yourself so you can watch the animals at work and rest!

Bird Abodes

No matter where you live, birds are one of the easiest wildlife visitors to attract. You may already have a lot of wild birds visiting your yard, especially if you're feeding them. Here are some easy ideas for encouraging them to be permanent visitors by building nests nearby. Then you can keep an eye out for busy parents feeding their young (an endless job!) or teaching the young birds to fly.

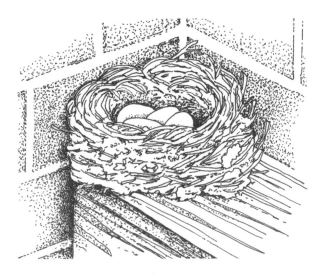

Nesting Preferences: Cavity or Platform?

Birds that nest in tree trunks, birdhouses, or other enclosed spaces are called *cavity nesters* — they like the confined, cozy space of a home with an entrance hole. Here are just a few of the birds in this group: woodpeckers, bluebirds, purple martins, nuthatches, titmice, wrens, chickadees, flycatchers, and some types of swallows. Offer them a cozy gourd birdhouse (pages 72 to 73) or make other special nesting boxes (see Resources, page 123).

Other birds, such as robins, mourning doves, blue jays, song sparrows, some swallows, house finches, and phoebes, are *platform nesters*. They build their nests in the eaves of buildings, in bushes and on branches, even smack over the trim on your doorway! (The robins at my house always seem to prefer the hanging planters, doorways, or even the top of the wind chimes to more natural abodes!) Invite these "open air" nesters with nesting materials (page 70) and a roomy spot to roost. Or, try the simple nesting lean-to (page 74) and see who moves in!

BARN SWALLOW

OSPREY

PIGEON NEST

Can You Spot the Nest?

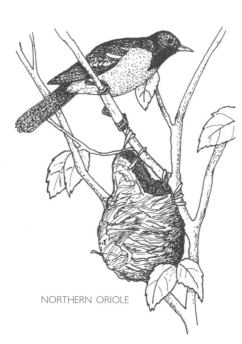

NORTHERN ORIOLE

In spring, look for birds making frequent trips with bits of twigs, grass, and other nesting materials. Can you see where they go?

Some birds prefer the woods; others like open fields and meadows. Look for concealed spots in trees and bushes and holes in dead trees. Certain birds, like juncos, are *ground nesters*, so don't overlook muddy banks and fallen logs, and the bases of trees and bushes. Many birds — pigeons, finches, sparrows, to name a few — are quite at home in densely populated urban areas. Watch for them carrying bits of paper or plastic amid the hustle and bustle of traffic. You can find nests under the eaves of buildings, beneath train trestles or bridges, in a tunnel or subway entrance, even on a public statue!

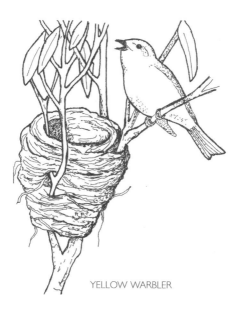

YELLOW WARBLER

"Help Yourself" Nest Supplies

In early spring, lend your feathered friends a hand by supplying an assortment of nest-building materials. Leave the supplies where they can be easily spotted. Some birds (robins, for example) use mud to "cement" their nests together, so a shallow pan filled with wet dirt or a patch of muddy ground will be appreciated, too! Then, keep an eye out for familiar bits of material in nests around your yard.

🍀 dried grass and moss

🍀 cut plant stems from old bouquets

🍀 short pieces of string and yarn ("un-knit" an old sweater or wool mittens)

🍀 stuffing from old furniture

🍀 cotton balls

🍀 dryer lint (save it in a plastic bag throughout the winter)

🍀 wood shavings

🍀 shredded paper

🍀 pet or people hair (from a recent brushing or trim)

🍀 cellophane "grass" from Easter baskets

🍀 short twigs

🍀 fabric scraps, cut into small strips

ROBIN AND NEST

Kids' Easy-to-Create Wildlife Habitats

Take a Closer Look

Construct a blind

Birds and other wildlife can be easily startled and may abandon their nesting sites if they are worried about what's around them. To keep them at ease, do what professional naturalists and photographers do — construct a blind!

If you have a tent, set it up where you can watch birds at your feeders or a nest under construction. Or, drive some stakes in the ground and drape an old blanket around them. Place branches and other foliage in front to keep it camouflaged and natural looking. Hide behind it at night, too, and see what critters come by!

A Gourd-geous Birdhouse

A dried gourd makes a cozy home for many different kinds of birds, and it will last for years. A gourd house hangs, swaying in the breeze, so it is less likely to be taken over by house sparrows and starlings or bothered by predators. It's easy to remember what kind of gourds to use: The ones for birdhouses are called *birdhouse gourds,* or sometimes *bottle* or *dipper gourds.* Look for them at farmstands or harvest markets in the fall (or grow your own!).

WHAT YOU NEED

Dried gourd

Bench vise

Drill, ¹/4" (5 mm) drill bit, a drill bit or
    speed bore for the size entrance hole
    you want or a small keyhole saw

String or wire (for hanging)

Varnish or paint

Paintbrush

Note: Please ask an adult for help
in using all of these tools.

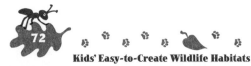

WHAT YOU DO

1. With an adult's help, secure the gourd in the vise and drill a hole through the top of the gourd. Drill several $^1/4$" (5 mm) drainage holes in the bottom, too. Drill or saw a round entrance hole in the upper third of the gourd (see COME ON IN!, below) and shake out the dried seeds.

2. Again with an adult's help, apply several coats of varnish to seal the outside. If you want to use the house for purple martins, paint it white. Brown or green is a good choice for other birds.

3. Hang the birdhouse from a tree branch or a horizontal wire with the opening away from the wind.

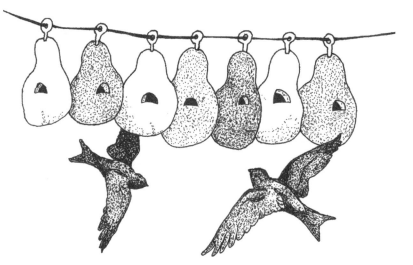

TO ATTRACT PURPLE MARTINS, HANG A GROUP OF GOURD HOUSES HIGH UP AND OUT IN THE OPEN. A CRESCENT-SHAPED HOLE IS BEST FOR KEEPING OUT STARLINGS.

Come on in!

Type of bird	Length of gourd	Entrance hole
Chickadee	6" (15 cm)	$1^1/2$" (3.5 cm)
Downy woodpecker	8" (20 cm)	$1^1/4$" (3 cm)
Hairy woodpecker	12" (30 cm)	$1^5/8$" (4 cm)
House wren	6" (15 cm)	1" (2.5 cm)
Nuthatch	8" (20 cm)	$1^1/4$" (3 cm)
Purple martin	10" (25 cm)	$2^1/2$" (6 cm)

Take a Closer Look

Nest etiquette

You don't ever want to bother a bird's nest in spring or summer, when it may be filled with eggs or otherwise in use. But because most birds build new nests every year, those same nests will likely be abandoned in fall.

Once the leaves have fallen off the trees in autumn, you may be able to see where many birds have cleverly positioned their nests and even to pick them up. Wear leather gloves to protect your hands as you carefully observe any nest. What did the bird use — twigs, grasses, bark? Is it woven together or cemented with mud? Do you see any of the nesting materials (page 70) you put out? Has any other animal, such as a mouse or insects, moved in? If so, leave it right where it is! Check in a field guide to see if you can discover what kind of bird lived in the nest.

Do-It-Yourself Nesting Lean-to

A simple wooden crate (ask for one in the produce section of the grocery store) with a lip added makes a super nest shelf for robins, phoebes, swallows, or other platform nesters. Or make a smaller shelf and tuck it under the shelter of a porch!

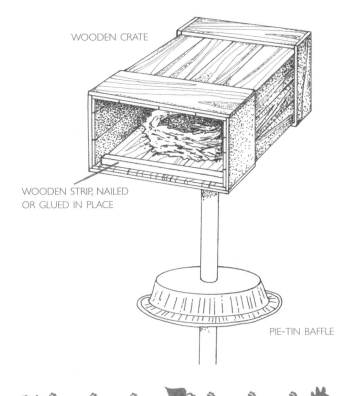

WOODEN CRATE

WOODEN STRIP, NAILED OR GLUED IN PLACE

PIE-TIN BAFFLE

Insect Hideaways!

Where do insects find food, shelter,
and protected spots to lay their eggs?
Just about everywhere!
Under and between rocks, under logs,
in scattered leaves, in the bark of trees,
in loose soil, in brush and weed piles —
these are all insect havens.
So if you're thinking that having
those places in your yard
will make it an insect-friendly habitat,
you're absolutely right!

LADYBUGS (REALLY A TYPE OF BEETLE) NESTLE
AMONG GRASS ROOTS OR ON GARDEN PLANTS
WHERE THEY MUNCH ON INSECTS.

Bees and Wasps: What's All the Buzz?

OK, I know you might not want to have bees or wasps too close for comfort. After all, they can sting! But the truth is, most bees and wasps have no intention of stinging you at all, and they are some of the hardest workers in orchards and gardens. Of course, they don't think of it as work — they're feeding on the sweet nectar. But as they busily buzz from flower to flower, they also carry some pollen along (it sticks to their feet). The more flowers that get pollinated, the more vegetables and fruits for us to enjoy. So bring on those bees!

Create a Home for Bees!

Planting foods bees like (page 55) is the best way to encourage them to come by, but a bee house might make them decide to stick around. Try these different nesting sites and see who moves in! Just be sure to set them in areas where they won't be disturbed and away from where you run and play.

Build a bee condo. Take a piece of scrap lumber or a log that's at least 3" (7.5 cm) thick. With an adult's help, drill holes 1/8" to 5/16" (2.5 to 6 mm) in diameter into it, spacing the holes about 1/2" to 3/4" (1 to 2 cm) apart and making them about 6" (15 cm) deep. Hang your bee condo under the eaves of your house or garden shed, protected from direct sun and rain.

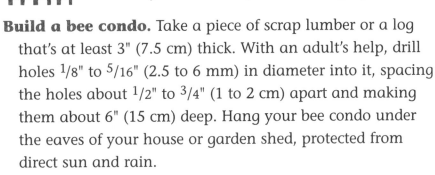

Try a bumble abode. In early spring, when bumblebees are looking for a home, help them out with an old flowerpot. Set it upside down in a quiet spot. In the wild, female bumblebees search out old mouse bedding and make their nests in it, so leave some lint or other soft bedding material inside the pot. To keep rain out of the hole, place a flat rock or a piece of wood over it, raising it slightly so that the bees can still get in.

Make a straw house. Tape a package of drinking straws together into a bundle, then plug one end of each straw with modeling clay, alternating back and forth so some openings face each way. Tape the straw house to the underside of an out-of-the-way windowsill.

Making a Difference

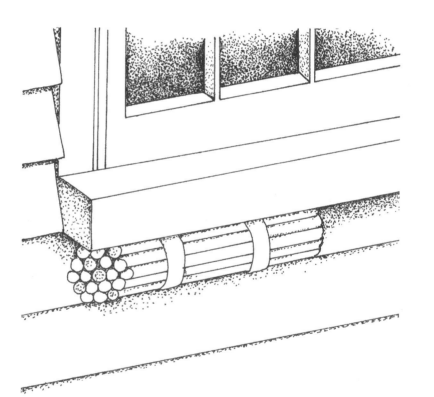

Welcome the Orchard Mason Bee!

Wanted: gentle but hardworking bee for pollination work.

Populations of wild bees are declining. Who's going to pollinate our fruits, vegetables, and flowers? Bumblebees have taken on some of that work, but here's another great candidate for the job! The orchard mason bee (found all over North America) is common in wooded areas but also turns up in cities and towns. It's small, black, and shiny, so it is sometimes mistaken for a fly.

A bee condo (page 76) will attract this small, gentle bee to your neighborhood. Place or hang it at least 3' (1 m) above ground, facing south or southeast. Keep a patch of muddy soil nearby so the bees can build the cell walls of the nest. Then, hang out quietly nearby and watch this little insect buzzing back and forth between its nest and nearby blossoms (it will make hundreds of trips in one day!). You'll see what "busy as a bee" really means!

ORCHARD MASON BEE
POLLINATING AN
APPLE BLOSSOM

Take a closer Look

Check out an empty wasp's nest

A nest made of paper? Sounds as if it would be flimsy, doesn't it? The gray, paperlike nests made by certain wasps and hornets are so strong, however, that you can often see them in fall and winter, still hanging from the eaves or between the branches of trees, despite the wind and rain and snow! The insect chews tiny pieces of wood, bark, and plants to create a pulp that looks sort of like papier-mâché.

In late fall or winter, when you are sure all the wasps and hornets are gone (check with an adult to be sure!), look at the nests up close. Do you see a honey-combed pattern? If the nest is entwined around several large branches in a tree, it's likely the nest of the bald-faced hornet. These wasps can be aggressive so have an adult determine that the nest is completely empty before you investigate it!

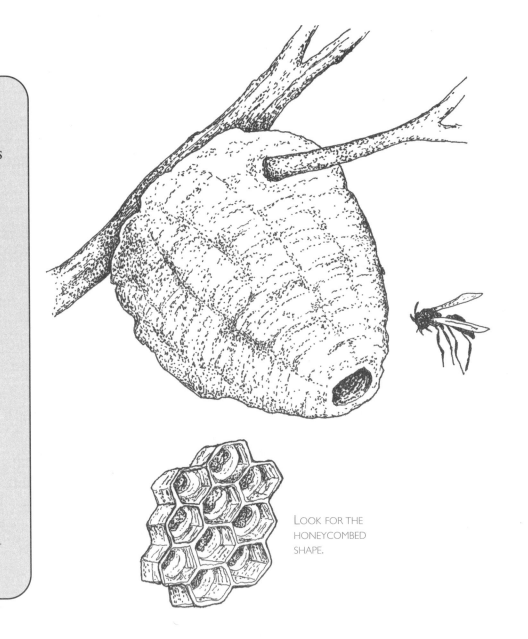

LOOK FOR THE HONEYCOMBED SHAPE.

Kids' Easy-to-Create Wildlife Habitats

Put Out a Mini-Insect Lodge!

 Create a miniature shelter for insects. All you need is a small log or a scrap of lumber. Place it on the ground and leave it undisturbed for a week. Then carefully peek underneath to see what's going on. Are any insects scurrying about? Leave the wood for two more weeks, then peek again. This time you might see ants at work. If the soil is moist, you might find centipedes, millipedes, sow bugs, or pill bugs. Have any mushrooms sprouted? Write down or record what you observe in your wildlife scrapbook (page 29).

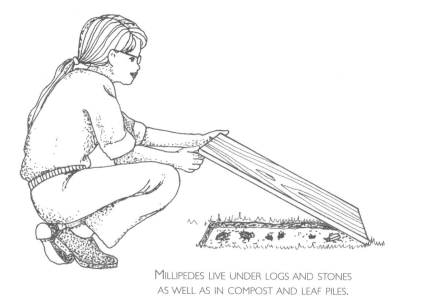

MILLIPEDES LIVE UNDER LOGS AND STONES AS WELL AS IN COMPOST AND LEAF PILES.

Take a Closer Look

An insect lived here!

One surefire clue that an insect visited a particular plant is a *gall*, a weird-looking lump that you sometimes see growing on a stem, leaf, bud, or bark. Galls usually start when a female fly, wasp, or other flying insect lays its eggs on a plant, or when the eggs hatch and the larvae begin feeding. The plant reacts to this activity by growing right over the insect, making a little protected spot for it. Then the insects eat their way out! (Nature sure creates some handy systems!) If you see exit holes in the gall, it means that the insects have already left. With an adult's help, open up the gall and explore the inside.

Make an Insect Observatory!

Many insects are so tiny and quick — and those that live in dark places don't like to be exposed to the light, so it can be difficult to see them up close. Here's how to "borrow" some from the wild for closer observation and keep them comfortable until you return them to their outdoor homes.

First, convince insects to come out of hiding with this easy-to-make contraption, known as a Berlese funnel.

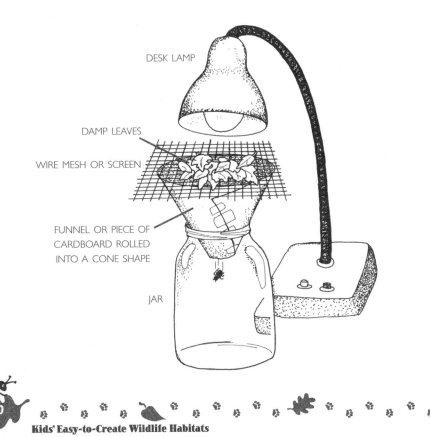

DESK LAMP

DAMP LEAVES

WIRE MESH OR SCREEN

FUNNEL OR PIECE OF
CARDBOARD ROLLED
INTO A CONE SHAPE

JAR

Place a handful of damp leaves and soil on the wire mesh or screen. The heat of the lamp will drive the insects and other critters through the mesh and into the jar below. If using a piece of window screen, poke or cut some holes in it to help the insects get through. Once the insects are in the jar, place the lid on (be sure to punch lots of tiny holes first to allow in air). Or, use a piece of screen secured with a rubber band. Include some fresh green leaves (sprinkled with water) for them to munch on, as well as a little dirt or dead leaves so they can be out of the light if they prefer.

Take a look at the insects you've captured. How many legs do they have? In what ways are they alike and different? When you are finished observing them, remember to return the insects to their proper homes!

Log Homes

You've seen log homes for people — why some of them have been around since Colonial days! But long before then, logs provided shelter for all sorts of critters, and they're still one of the most popular animal homes, especially for insects. But here's the key to a really good log home for critters: The more *rotten* it is, the better!

Huh, you say? A *rotten* log? Aren't logs for buildings supposed to be firm and sturdy? You're right if you're thinking of people homes. Those logs do have to be solid and dry. But for many critters, that newly fallen log only becomes interesting as it starts to decay. It's all part of nature's process of *decomposition*.

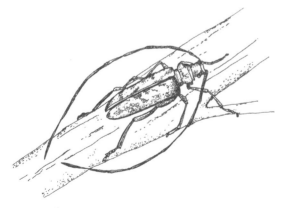

A BARK-EATING BEETLE AT WORK ON A TREE.

Take a closer Look

Explore a rotting log

First, find a log that's not actively being used as a home for wildlife that you wouldn't want to disturb (bees and other stinging insect or snakes, for example). Now close your eyes and use your other senses to find out what's going on.

Listen as you tap the log. Does it sound solid or hollow?

Feel the outside. Is it hard or soft, rough or smooth, wet or dry?

Smell the log. Does it smell musty or wet or more like dry firewood?

Now, open your eyes and do some more exploring. Carefully pull some of the log apart, using a magnifying glass to examine what's inside. Look under and on top of the log, too. What critters do you see? Check out the log hotel and restaurant on page 82 for more clues about where to look. Can you find a few more log-loving creatures?

When you are finished investigating, return the log and its contents to where you found it, so the animal shelter will still be there!

Is It Soil Soup Yet?

Don't worry, that log you are looking at won't go away while you blink, but there's a good chance it won't be there 10 years from now. That's about how long it takes a dead tree to turn into soil, depending on where you live and the type of tree and climate you have. As different plants and animals make their homes in a rotting log, they eat the log, or dig in it, or even eat each other! (Wild critters are not very responsible houseguests, are they?) So, eventually, no more log shelter and snack bar. But it has replenished a whole new habitat, one that's home to insects, earthworms, and more — the soil!

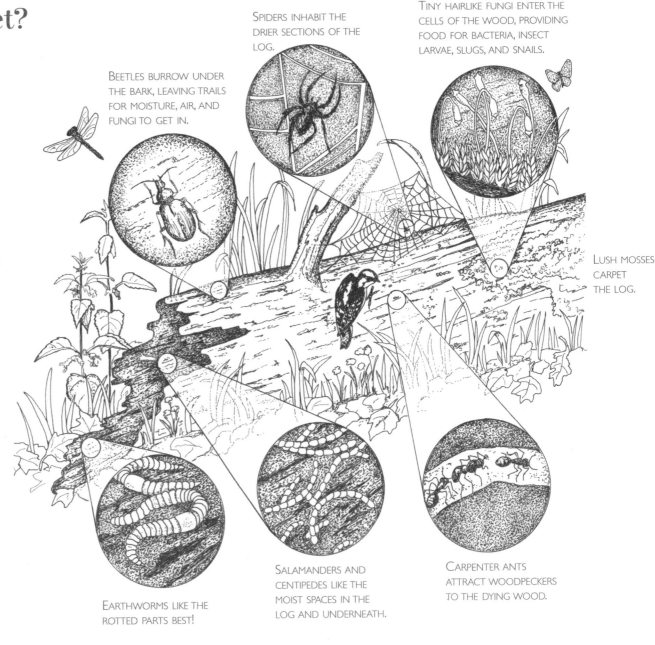

SPIDERS INHABIT THE DRIER SECTIONS OF THE LOG.

TINY HAIRLIKE FUNGI ENTER THE CELLS OF THE WOOD, PROVIDING FOOD FOR BACTERIA, INSECT LARVAE, SLUGS, AND SNAILS.

BEETLES BURROW UNDER THE BARK, LEAVING TRAILS FOR MOISTURE, AIR, AND FUNGI TO GET IN.

LUSH MOSSES CARPET THE LOG.

EARTHWORMS LIKE THE ROTTED PARTS BEST!

SALAMANDERS AND CENTIPEDES LIKE THE MOIST SPACES IN THE LOG AND UNDERNEATH.

CARPENTER ANTS ATTRACT WOODPECKERS TO THE DYING WOOD.

Do you recognize some of these tenants who live in a log?

The log-eaters: These guys are officially called the *primary consumers*, which is just a fancy way of saying that they eat the log itself. Termites, carpenter ants, wood borers, click beetles, bark beetles, engraver beetles, *fungi* (a group of plants that includes mushrooms and molds), and bacteria all share this feast!

The log-eater eaters:

These critters, technically called the *secondary consumers*, munch on the log-eaters. Here's where your centipedes, daddy longlegs, wolf spiders, mites, ants, salamanders, and woodpeckers get to work.

A HOLLOW LOG IS A PERFECT HOME FOR RACCOONS, TOO!

The scavengers: Dead remains of plants and critters make a fine meal for these rot-loving beasts, also called the *decomposers*. They break down the wood into soil. Millipedes, pill bugs, wood roaches, snails, earthworms, mites, and slugs happily feast away! For more on earthworms, including a close-up look at the critical soil improvements they make, see page 84.

Play Log Tag

Choose one person to be It. That person tries to tag the others, who must squat down and call out the name of a creature that lives in, on, or under a rotting log, or else they become It. No repeat names allowed!

Take a Closer Look

Observe earthworms at work!

Investigate earthworms at work with this simple setup of an earthworm habitat. Fill a large, widemouth glass jar with layers of garden soil, peat moss, and sand. Water thoroughly. Add some worms from the ground, scattering them over the surface. Cover with some dead leaves or grass clippings. Then cover the jar with a dark cloth or a paper bag and place it in a cool place. Don't screw the lid back on — your worms need oxygen.

After a while, check your worms. Do you see how the layers shift as the worms tunnel through the soil? Look for ripples of soil on the surface. These are the *castings*, made when earthworms eat the soil and eliminate it through their bodies. When you are finished watching the worms, carefully return them to their outdoor homes, where they can continue working the soil. Use the nutrient-rich soil the worms created to feed some plants!

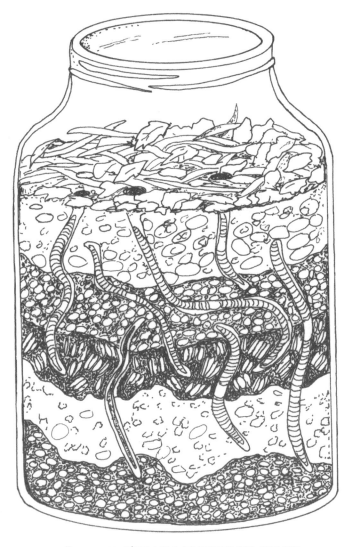

EARTHWORMS' TUNNELS AERATE THE SOIL AND LET RAINWATER MOVE THROUGH IT AS WELL, SUPPLYING PLANT ROOTS AND SOIL-DWELLING INSECTS WITH OXYGEN.

Welcome Some Wigglers!

Here's some wildlife you *can* keep indoors as pets — about 1,000 or so to be exact! Set up an indoor worm box to feed and shelter some red wiggler worms. It doesn't take much space, and these quiet little creatures spend their days munching on your kitchen scraps, much the way outdoor worms help consume a decaying log.

They're a great way to see the soil-enrichment process up close, if you live where decaying logs aren't so easy to find or during the winter, when soil-dwellers aren't as active. And the bonus is, you'll have free fertilizer (the castings) to feed your houseplants, window boxes, or garden!

WHAT YOU NEED

Drill (for use with adult help)

Wooden or plastic bin (no more than 1 1/2'/45 cm deep) with a lid

1" (2.5 cm) strips of old newspaper

Small amount of soil

Water

Red wiggler worms (page 87)

Wooden blocks

Large sheet of plastic or several layers of old newspaper

Note: A 2' x 3' x 1' container (60 x 90 x 30 cm) is a great size for the kitchen waste from a family of four.

WHAT YOU DO
TO PREPARE THE WORMS' BED

1. With an adult's help, drill 10 or 12 holes in the bottom of the bin for drainage and airflow. (Don't worry; the worms won't escape!)

2. Fill the bin about three-fourths full of newspaper strips; add a handful of soil (to provide grit in the worm's gizzard so it can digest its food). Mix everything together and moisten it, letting the water soak in. The bedding should be damp but not soaking wet. Squeeze a handful — if you get more than a few drops of water, pour off the excess or let the box dry out a bit.

3. Place the box on wooden blocks (for air circulation) with plastic or newspapers underneath it, where the air temperature will be between 55° and 77°F (13° to 25°C).

4. Place the worms in the box and watch them start to head down where it's dark and damp! Then put the lid on.

TO FEED THE WORMS

A pound (500 g) of red wigglers (about 1,000 worms) will eat about three pounds (1.5 kg) of food a week. You can feed them fruit and vegetable scraps, coffee grounds, tea leaves, crushed eggshells (for calcium) — even those "science projects" from the back of the fridge are OK. Avoid meat, dairy products, and oily foods. Add small amounts of food each day, placing them in different sections of the bin.

TO REMOVE THE CASTINGS

Your worms are like tiny composting bins: The food scraps and bedding go in one end, and dark, crumbly castings (everything the worm doesn't digest) come out the other end. The castings are actually poisonous to the worms, so it's important to remove them about once a month. And it's fun! You'll see!

1. Spread out the contents of the bin on the plastic sheet or newspapers. Remove the top layer of bedding and let the worms move down to escape the light. Separate out the dark, crumbly castings. Keep removing the top layer and waiting a minute or so, until you're left with a pile of worms. See if you spot any of the small round cocoons, which can contain up to 20 eggs (although usually only three or four worms hatch). The cocoons turn red when the worms are ready to wiggle out.

2. Put the worms, a few cocoons, and the bedding back in the bin and you're ready to roll! Add fresh bedding and a little more soil about every four months.

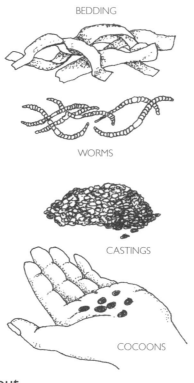

BEDDING

WORMS

CASTINGS

COCOONS

Habitat Questions ... With Answers!

I brought in worms from outdoors and observed them in a jar (page 80). Why can't I keep those worms in my worm box?

Most of the worms you find in the yard or garden prefer cooler temperatures than you could easily provide in your worm box. It's OK to observe them for a short time in the jar, but then they need to go back outdoors. Plus, those worms are likely to be *earthmovers*, which prefer to eat soil.

For a worm box, you want *composting worms* — these guys like to hang out in a big group eating plants and turning them into castings. *Red wigglers* (also called *redworms* or *manure worms*) are a composting worm that will live very happily in a worm box. They are easy to raise and can survive in a wide range of temperatures. You can buy red wigglers at a bait store (where they might be called *dungworms* or *striped worms*). Or, you can order them from mail-order sources (see Resources, page 123).

Make a Compost Pile

Why would an earth-friendly kid like you toss out kitchen scraps when you could turn them into compost (or black gold, as a lot of gardeners call it because it's so good for the soil!)? *Compost* is the end result of a natural process that turns fruit and vegetable scraps, grass clippings, leaves, and pieces of plants into nutrient-rich soil. Plus, a compost pile provides homes and food for scavengers like worms, grubs, and lots of tiny microscopic critters like fungi and bacteria!

Composting does *not* mean just throwing all your vegetable scraps in a pile in the backyard. A successful compost pile requires a little attention. But even if you have only a small spot in your backyard, you can compost.

Pick a site. First, decide where you're going to put your compost pile. An out-of-the-way spot near the garden or house is best — if the pile is too far away, you probably won't take care of it. A level spot, close to a water spigot or hose, is ideal.

Choose the enclosure. If you live in the city, an enclosed bin is best, because it will keep out unwanted critters and will look nice and neat. You can buy plastic bins at garden centers or make your own by punching holes in the sides and bottom of a 50-gallon (185 L) drum.

You can also make an enclosure out of chicken wire and stakes, or build a simple wooden bin with slats of wood. You'll probably notice birds visiting your compost pile, looking for tasty treats. But if other animals (like neighborhood dogs) start "digging in," you'll need to secure a piece of wire on top for a lid. Make the bin about a yard (m) wide and tall. That way, you'll have a big enough pile of stuff that will actually heat up in the middle but at the same time, it will still get lots of air in it. The combination of heat and air is what helps speed the breakdown of plant matter into soil.

Make the mix. Start your pile with a 4" or 6" (10 or 15 cm) layer of leaves, loose soil, twigs, and other yard trimmings. On top of that, add a mixture of "green" and "brown" plant materials and scraps. The "greens" are fresh and include vegetable peels, stale bread, tea bags, coffee grounds, grass clippings, eggshells, and other fresh materials. Include a sprinkling of composted cow manure (available from a hardware store or garden center). The "browns" are dry and dead plants like straw, wood chips, twigs, even some shredded newspaper. Don't include meat or fish scraps, dairy products, or grease or fat in your pile (they all attract pests); also avoid pet wastes or cat litter, diseased plants, weeds with seeds, or wood that's been treated with pesticides or other chemicals.

A good rule for quick compost is to have one part "green" stuff to three parts "brown." Make the layers, then wet the pile with water so that it is about as moist as a damp kitchen sponge. Cover the pile with a trash bag or tarp, or even an old rug.

BROWN

GREEN

BROWN
(TWIGS, SOIL,
AND YARD
TRIMMINGS)

Turn, turn, turn. Let the pile sit for a few weeks, then water it and "turn" it with a pitchfork or garden spade to add air to the pile and move the moisture around. Don't be surprised if you see lots of worms — they're part of the process and are just doing their job! Let the compost sit again, then turn it again, and so on (this process will take about three months or more) until it is a dark crumbly material that even smells good (honest!). That's compost!

Kids to the Rescue!

Make the most of compost!

Composting is one of the best things you can do to improve your habitat. For starters, you're not throwing away all that stuff. If more folks composted, it would keep *tons* of food and yard waste from filling up local landfills.

What's more, finished compost is great for raising plants of all kinds. You can sprinkle it around in your vegetable garden, or around the base of trees and shrubs, in flower beds and window boxes, you name it. It's like giving your plants a vitamin boost!

All Kinds of Wildlife!

A flat rock, some sticks and brush, a piece of pipe
— these are the simple tools you need
to attract critters from salamanders, lizards,
and toads to shrews, chipmunks, and rabbits.
Once you know what to use (and why)
and how to arrange it,
you can create a wildlife resort!

Habitat Questions ... With Answers!

People in our neighborhood like things to look neat. Won't creating a "wild" spot for wildlife or a shelter of sticks just look messy?

First of all, a wildlife habitat will make your yard look *more* cared for, not less! Yes, your neighbors might well object to a pile of brush tossed in a heap in the backyard. But most likely they won't have a problem with a neatly arranged stack of sticks topped with evergreen branches in a protected corner of the yard (pages 92 to 93), a carefully arranged log or two surrounded by bark mulch with a toad house nearby (page 97), or artfully placed flat rocks with butterfly-friendly wildflowers growing around them (page 94).

In fact, your neighbors just might be so intrigued by all the life and color they see next door that they'll want to copy what you do to attract wildlife to their yards, too!

Build a Wildlife Shelter

 A pile of sticks and twigs? Take a closer look. It's a wildlife brush shelter. See how it's carefully arranged? After all, the insects and small animals that will hang out in there need air, and water, and you certainly don't want the pile to collapse on top of them as they move about inside! It might not look too comfortable to you, but to many animals — from small mammals to lizards, toads, and snakes, as well as songbirds and butterflies — it's the Ritz! It provides a secure hiding place as well as some welcome snacks, such as the tiny insects in the soil or the decaying wood.

Build your shelter in an out-of-the way corner of your yard. It can be as big or as small as you want. Gather sticks, tree trimmings, leaves, and weeds. (A great time to do this is after a heavy rain or windy day, when there are lots of fallen twigs and sticks on the lawn.) Start with a base of larger, thicker logs and sticks. An old pipe or two in or near the base will provide cool, dark hiding spots for snakes, lizards, and toads. Add the smaller materials in layers. Top the pile with leaves, grass clippings, or weeds for a thatched-roof effect. You want a sturdy pile that provides hiding places and plenty of room for "scrambling around" inside. A pile about 2' (60 cm) high is ideal for larger animals, but even a small brush pile helps out insects and other tiny wildlife.

Record Animals and Bird Sounds!

Use a portable cassette player, or a video camera. If you can, have a portable microphone so you can get closer to animal sounds without being seen. Attach the microphone to the end of a broomstick, or put it in the crook of a tree. What sounds do you pick up? Can you guess what any might be?

93

Roll Out the Rocks!

Do you have a collection of favorite rocks? Don't forget to place a few of them in your wildlife habitats! Cold-blooded reptiles (page 15) like snakes, lizards, and *geckos* (a type of lizard found in parts of the South and Southwest) love to bask on flat rocks because they hold the sun's heat. And these creatures can quickly slip out of sight between larger rocks if they need a hiding spot.

GARTER SNAKES SUN THEMSELVES DURING THE DAY. THEY WON'T HURT YOU OR YOUR PETS!

LIZARDS DART INTO CRACKS BETWEEN ROCKS FOR SHELTER.

Butterflies and dragonflies also rest on sun-warmed rocks (and sip from the water that collects in their nooks and crannies). A small pile of rocks, set loosely on top of one another, is a handy hiding spot for a chipmunk, toad, or snake. Beetles, spiders, bees, and other insects will hang out in there, too!

Leave the Leaves, Please!

Instead of putting raked leaves out with the trash (or — even worse — burning them, which pollutes the air), leave some under bushes and low-growing plants to provide food and shelter for animals. If you play in the leaves first, they'll crumble into tiny pieces and then break down even faster, providing food for soil-dwelling critters! Put the rest in a neat pile where they'll provide welcome shelter for animals or insects. Around the base of a "sidewalk" tree is a great spot — it conserves the moisture in the soil and will slowly feed the tree over time! (For more ideas on helping these often neglected trees, see page 28.) You may notice that some animals, such as raccoons and squirrels, have moved leaves high up in the tree branches to make comfy nests.

Make a Squirrel Nesting Box

Help red and gray squirrels to find a cozy winter home by offering them a nesting box. Squirrels use at least three dens when they are raising their young, and sometimes as many as seven! They prefer deep holes in tree trunks, but if they can't find them, they'll appreciate finding this wooden box vacant. And if a squirrel doesn't move in, bees or songbirds just might instead when spring comes!
For plans for a box,
see Resources, page 123.

Kids to the Rescue!

Save a snag

Save a what? A *snag!* It's another name for a dead tree that is left standing. In the wild, these old trees are prime real estate! Many birds nest in the soft wood in dead trees, and insects, amphibians, small mammals, and insects all rely on snags for food and shelter. Hawks and owls like to perch at the top (great view while hunting!), and woodpeckers and other birds feast on the many insects eating the wood.

With open land becoming more developed, many of these old trees are being cut down. Tell your parents and others in your neighborhood about how important snags are and explain how it helps *many* different types of wildlife if we leave these dead trees standing right where they are (unless, of course, they are in danger of falling on houses or people).

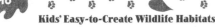

Kids' Easy-to-Create Wildlife Habitats

Toads Welcome Here!

 Toads are rather shy, quiet creatures. To improve your chances of observing one of these amphibians (page 15) in your yard, provide a cool, moist, shady shelter for it. Here are two types to try. (For more on attracting toads and other amphibians, see JUST ADD WATER, pages 99 to 120.)

USE AN OVERTURNED FLOWERPOT. TO MAKE A DOORWAY, PROP UP THE EDGE OF THE POT ON SMALL ROCKS.

BURY A FLOWERPOT OR CAN PARTWAY IN MOIST SOIL.

Is there a protected spot near an outdoor light where you can put your toad house? In the evening, the light will attract bugs and the toad can hang out and munch away! Place a saucer of water nearby, in case it gets thirsty. (Don't be surprised if you see the toad sitting in the saucer — it drinks by absorbing the water through its skin!) Or, try a toad house near your WILDLIFE BRUSH SHELTER (pages 92 to 93) or the WILDLIFE MINI-MOTEL (page 25).

Simple Shelters: Home, Sweet Home for Animal Friends

Be a Bat Watcher!

Let's face it — bats, those famous flying mammals (page 15), have a bad reputation! But if it weren't for bats, we'd each have *a lot* more insect bites. A single brown bat can catch as many as 600 mosquitoes in one hour, or 7,000 mosquitoes in one night!

All the bats in North America are *nocturnal* (active at night). Take a walk on a warm still summer night at dusk. If you can walk near a pond or marsh, that's even better — lots of flying insects there. Watch above you for bats swooping and dipping. Don't worry, they're not interested in coming near you — they're after all those tasty insects!

Kids to the Rescue!

Go to bat for bats!

Almost half of the bat species found in North America are considered to be threatened or endangered. One of the best ways to encourage bats to stick around and become your private mosquito-munchers is to offer them a bat house where they can sleep during the day. Bats are fussy about their roosting spots, however.

For the specifics on building and positioning a bat house, see Resources, page 123. Remember, bats need your help!

Just Add Water!
Sips, Dips, Puddles & Ponds

All wild animals need water to survive, just as you and your pets do. Sure, you know ducks like the water, but butterflies and dragonflies, birds, moles, squirrels, and rabbits need it too. Some animals, like toads and other amphibians, even spend part of their lives in the water, while others need water for drinking and for keeping clean. (Yes, wild animals take baths!)

To most critters, though, your yard probably looks more like a desert than an inviting oasis. Buildings and walkways, terraces, and concrete playgrounds — even yards covered with grass — just don't offer many choices for sipping or dipping. And roads and highways can make it difficult or dangerous for animals like frogs and salamanders to travel safely to their favorite watery spots.

How can you help? Offer them a source of cool, refreshing water to sip, drink, use for bathing, and even live in! Making a watery retreat for the wildlife around you is easier than you think.

Bathing Is for the Birds (and Other Critters, Too!)

Have you ever seen birds flitting in puddles after a rainstorm? Many birds bathe as part of their daily preening ritual to keep their feathers in top shape. Birds will even try to bathe in and drink from the water that collects on plants with big cupped leaves, like hostas. Some birds "leaf bathe" by fluttering among the wet leaves of trees and shrubs. Beckon them all with an easy-to-make birdbath!

HANGING FRISBEE BIRDBATH

SHALLOW PAN ON A STUMP

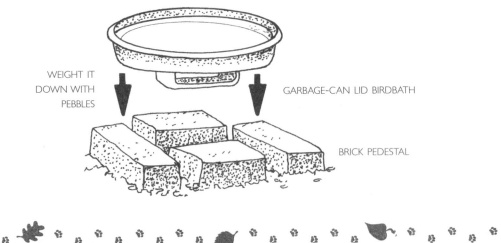

WEIGHT IT DOWN WITH PEBBLES

GARBAGE-CAN LID BIRDBATH

BRICK PEDESTAL

Splish, Splish, Taking a Bath!

A birdbath can be as simple as a stone with a depression in it, or a saucer or pan of water. Or, try a garbage-can lid turned upside down with pebbles in it to weight it down and give the critters firm footing.

PLANT SAUCER ON A PLASTIC CRATE

Puddle Perfection

A simple depression in the ground that stays moist can be a natural wildlife watering hole. Some birds, such as thrushes, even prefer a ground-level spot that's hidden under tree cover, so that they can drop down and bathe unnoticed. Butterflies and moths like to gather on muddy areas to get a drink and rabbits, toads, insects, and garden snails will also appreciate this moist retreat. Fill your puddle with water from a garden hose during dry weather.

Wildlife Water Safety

Keep it shallow. Birds are wary of water that is more than 2" to 3" (5 to 6 cm) deep. Arrange a few branches or stones in the water so that birds can stand on them and drink without getting their feet wet. In summer, these "islands" will help waterlogged bugs, especially bees, climb to safety so they can fly away. A securely attached twig that sticks out of the water at the edge also makes a good landing spot.

Add a beach. Do you like to ease into the water at the beach or swimming pool or jump right in? Many small animals prefer the cautious approach. So for deeper birdbaths or watering holes at ground level, make sure at least one side has sand or pebbles so that birds and other critters can enter the water slowly, without slipping too far in. To give them an "escape ladder," stretch a piece of window screen or garden netting up over the side of the bath.

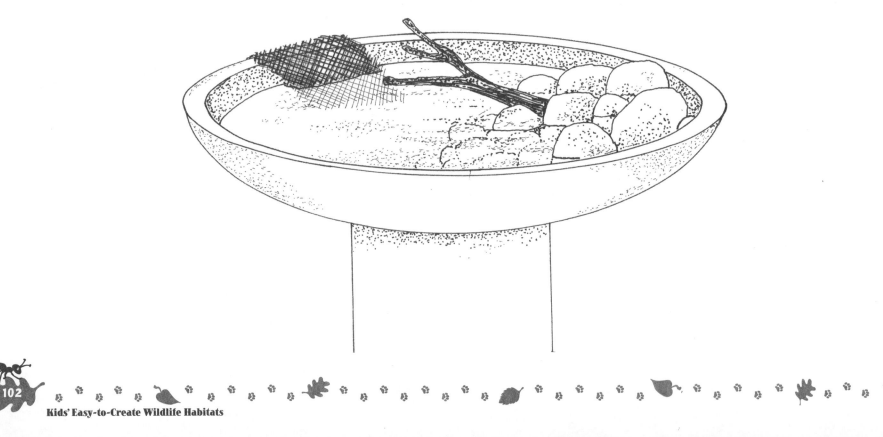

Vary the location. Many birds prefer to bathe 2' to 3' (60 to 90 cm) off the ground in a clearing, with trees or shrubs 5' to 15' (1.5 to 4.5 m) away, so that they can keep an eye out for cats and other predators yet quickly fly to cover. Other birds, like warblers, prefer to bathe in denser shrubbery at ground level. And rabbits and toads definitely need a ground-level bathing spot. To attract the most wildlife, offer several types of bathing options.

Clean the tub. Remember, birds and other animals need *clean* water. Check the water regularly and empty and scrub out the birdbaths every two to three days, especially in warmer weather when algae growth and mosquito larvae are more apt to be a problem (see HABITAT QUESTIONS … WITH ANSWERS!, page 104). A green scum on the bottom is a sure sign that cleaning is overdue! Never use kitchen or bathroom cleaners in your animal baths, though, as the chemicals in the cleaners may harm the very animals you're trying to attract.

Water in Winter

Water can be especially hard for animals to find in winter when streams and ponds are frozen over. Check the water in your birdbath or shallow garden pool daily to be sure it hasn't iced up. (Never add antifreeze; it's poisonous to all animals, including you.) Even in winter, be sure to clean out the birdbath regularly to keep it safe for drinking and bathing.

Habitat Questions ... With Answers!

The past few summers I've heard my parents talking with the neighbors about something called West Nile virus. One neighbor even got rid of her birdbath, saying that it might attract the mosquitoes that carry this disease. What is West Nile virus, and is it really OK to put a birdbath in our yard?

I can see why you might be confused. Your neighbor got rid of her birdbath, and this book is suggesting you add one. Hey, which is the right thing to do? Well, the good news is that you can safely have a birdbath in your yard, or even a small garden pool or pond (pages 107 to 108).

The West Nile virus first showed up in the United States in 1999. The virus is carried by many species of birds. Mosquitoes then carry the disease from birds to people (mosquitoes bite an infected bird and then bite a person). So the key to controlling this disease is to keep mosquito populations under control (a good thing to do anyway!).

Mosquitoes lay their eggs in standing (nonmoving) water — birdbaths, ponds, rain barrels, and such. The trick is to keep the water moving and to clean away any mosquito larvae before they hatch. As long as you keep your birdbath and any other containers of water that you have put out for wildlife clean and change the water every couple of days, they won't turn into mosquito factories. Once a week, flush the birdbath thoroughly with the hose and then refill.

Another option is buy a battery-operated water agitator for your birdbath or mount a dripper or a mister to create a fine spray. (It will probably attract even more birds to your birdbath — birds *love* moving water.) For larger areas of water such as ponds, consider treating the water with nontoxic *larvicide* (it kills the larvae) that is safe for fish, plants, and people. (See Resources, page 123.)

Another precaution you can take to protect yourself against West Nile virus is to wear long pants and long-sleeved shirts and use insect repellent at the times of day when mosquitoes are most active (early morning and at dusk).

Take a Closer Look

Life at the baths

Watch what comes to your birdbath, checking at different times of day. Are there certain times of day that the birds like to bathe best, or do they visit all day long? Where do they like to stand while they're drinking or bathing? See if you can spy insects "skating" or walking across the surface of the water, moths flitting at the edge, or bees alighting for a drink. Head outdoors with a flashlight and see what's going on at night, too.

PUT UP A RAIN BARREL OR BUCKET TO CAPTURE RAINWATER FOR CRITTERS (AND GARDEN PLANTS, TOO!).

Pondside Adventures (Wherever You Live!)

No doubt about it, animals —
and people! — are drawn to ponds
and small pools of water. So including one
in your backyard habitat will bring
water-loving wildlife you might not
otherwise see. No matter how small
a homemade pond is, it offers a refreshing
oasis, even in the middle of the city.
And combined with blooming flowers
or other greenery, and a little fountain,
a mini-pond is just about irresistable
to backyard critters as a spot
to drink or dip.

ALMOST ANY OUTDOOR SPACE CAN OFFER A COOL,
REFRESHING SPOT TO WILDLIFE.

Build a Backyard Mini-Pond

Does adding a pond sound like a big job? It's really quite simple, if you put in a miniature one. Don't worry — you won't need a bulldozer! You can fit a mini-pond in even the smallest yard. Your pond can be as simple as a small plastic wading pool or a large metal container sunk into the ground, or the more "deluxe" model shaped with black plastic shown here. (Just be sure to get permission first before you start digging!)

WHAT YOU NEED
6' to 8' (1.8 to 2.5 m) of rope
Shovel
Large piece of thick plastic or old tarp
Stones or bricks

WHAT YOU DO
Outline a pond shape you like with the rope. Keep the curves simple and soft so that you won't have tricky corners to work with. A pond about 6' (1.8 m) in diameter and 16" (40 cm) deep will hold a variety of animals and be cooler for frogs and fish, but a small 2' by 3' (60 by 90 cm) pond (or even a 4-gallon/16 L container) can work well.

Dig out a sloping hole, making sure to have a shallow "beach" so animals and birds can ease in and out of the water and a level edge all around for plants to grow. Smooth out any rough areas, removing rocks that might poke through, adding sand if needed to cushion the bottom.

Not too Sunny, not too Shady

The best spot for a pond is in an area that gets part sun and part shade. Too much shade and leaf cover will make the water dark and full of decaying leaves, while too much sun encourages *algae* — those tiny green plants that form a scummy film in the water.

Cover the hole with the thick plastic. (You can buy heavy-duty plastic at garden centers and hardware stores or even special pond liners.) Anchor the edges with stones or bricks and add a larger stone island. Fill the pond with water.

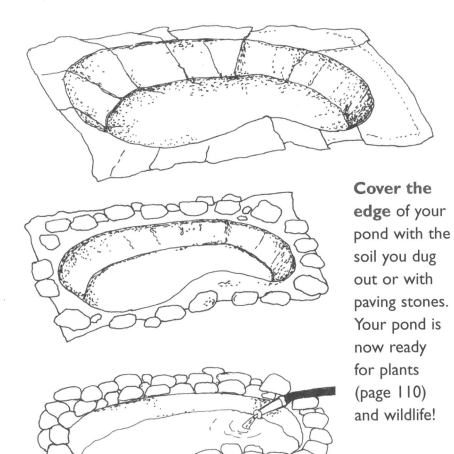

Cover the edge of your pond with the soil you dug out or with paving stones. Your pond is now ready for plants (page 110) and wildlife!

Add a Fountain

Moving water will attract even more wildlife to your backyard habitat. (Hummingbirds especially like the spray from running water — they'll fly right through it to take a quick shower.) To make a mini-waterfall in your pond or birdbath, punch a tiny hole in the bottom of an old bucket or plastic container. Fill it with water and set it on rocks at the edge of the pond (or hang it above the birdbath) so the water drips out slowly. Ah, how refreshing!

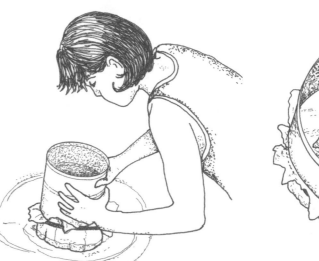

Pond Plantings

Flowers blooming at the edge of your pond
will make it more attractive to
you and to wildlife! Yellow flag iris, for
example, loves to have its feet wet and
thrives right at the water's edge.
Ferns and clumps of tall grasses offer
shade and shelter for small critters
that come to drink. For other
easy-to-grow perennials,
see page 55.

Make an Underwater Viewer

Curious to see what's going on in the water without diving in? Try this!

Remove the top and bottom of a large, empty can (a coffee can works well!) and carefully cover any sharp edges with duct tape. Then stretch plastic wrap across the top, using a wide rubber band to hold it in place. Pull gently on the sides of the plastic to make a tight seal. To use, just lower the plastic wrapped end into the water and catch a clear view of whatever lies below the surface!

Take a Closer Look

Explore a pond, stream, or wetland

Even if you live in the city, it's likely there are some watery places that you can explore with an adult. You'll be amazed at all the creatures you can find, once you know where to look! You may catch a glimpse of a long-legged heron wading in the quiet water or a painted turtle basking on a rock in the sun. In autumn, keep an eye out for migrating geese taking a well-deserved rest. Here are some tips for exploring.

Dress for wet conditions (old sneakers or wading boots), and apply plenty of insect repellent to keep away mosquitoes and other biting insects (this is *their* habitat, after all).

Bring an insect net (pages 112 to 113), binoculars, and a magnifying glass so you can get a closer look at things, as well as some collection jars for taking water samples or looking up close at insects and other critters. You might even want to bring a tape recorder for recording bird songs or frogs croaking.

Most important, *never* go to ponds, lakes, brooks, or rivers without an adult — and no exceptions! Thank you. (Safety always comes first, even when you're having fun in nature.)

Many creatures stay hidden and still in the heat of the day, so the best time to visit is in the early morning or at dusk, approaching quietly so that you don't disturb the wildlife or scare them away.

Look for tracks along the water's edge or in the mud and for nests in trees or shrubs. On the water's surface, look for plants floating, insects walking, and the ripples where fish or other creatures come up to the surface. At the edge or in the muck, poke around for signs of insect larvae, worms, and floating frog, toad, or fish eggs. What else do you observe? What ideas does this natural habitat give you for your mini-pond at home?

Race as "Fast" as a Turtle

If you come upon a turtle basking on a sunny rock in a pond, you might be surprised at how *quickly* it can slip into the water if it hears you approaching. Most of the time, however, turtles are slowpokes. And if they sense danger while on land, they typically stop moving altogether, pull their legs and heads into their shells, and wait it out.

Challenge your friends to a turtle race! Move as *s-l-o-w-l-y* as you can (no stopping allowed, though) — the last one to the finish line wins!

Do-It-Yourself Insect Net

Watery spots are an insect paradise. But flying insects are difficult to observe — they just fly away too quickly! To get a better view, make your own net. To close it once you've caught something, quickly twist the handle. Don't worry — the net won't hurt the insects, and you'll let them go as soon as you've had a close look.

WHAT YOU NEED

Wire coat hanger
Strong tape
Broomstick or thick dowel
Measuring tap

Scissors
Nylon netting
Needle and thread
Strip of cotton fabric

WHAT YOU DO

1. Straighten the coat hanger hook; then tape the hanger's hook to the broomstick, wrapping it tightly. Bend the rest of the hanger into a circle.

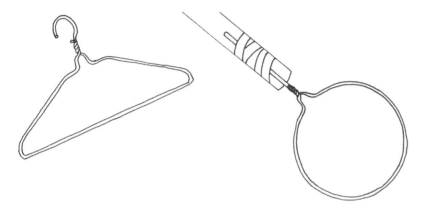

2. Measure around the wire. Cut the netting into a large W shape as shown, with the straight edge the same measurement as the wire circle.

THIS EDGE SHOULD FIT THE WIRE CIRCLE.

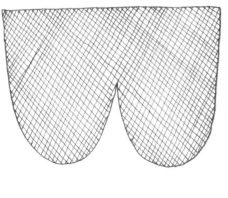

3. Sew a 3"-wide (7.5 cm) strip of fabric to the straight edge of the net, then sew the sides together.

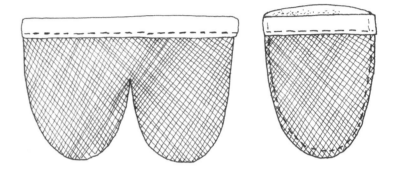

4. Attach the bag to the frame by folding the cotton strip over the wire and sewing it back to itself.

Desert Drinkers

Animals in the desert have a special challenge — getting drinking water in a very dry habitat where a stream or water hole might not be handy for many miles (km). Let's see how they find water to quench their thirst.

WHAT YOU NEED
Small shovel
Patch of very dry, sandy soil or large bucket of sand
Paper cup
Small stones
Large piece of plastic wrap

WHAT YOU DO

1. In a sunny area, dig a 2' (60 cm) hole in the ground or in the bucket. Set up the cup, stones, and plastic wrap as shown.

2. After a few hours, check it out. Are there drops of water on the underside of the plastic? Has any water dripped into the cup?

Here's what's going on: The sun heats up any moisture in the sand or soil, and that water *evaporates* (turns from liquid to a vapor) into the air. When the water vapor touches the plastic wrap, it *condenses* (turns back to liquid). So it may seem as though there isn't any water in dry desert soil, but if animals dig down, they will find some! But you can sure make life easier for your wildlife friends by providing some refreshing sipping spots in your yard.

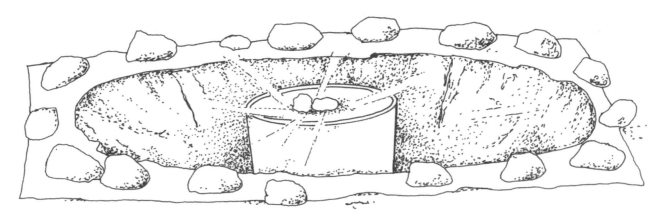

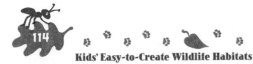

Fun With Frogs and Friends

GIANT CALIFORNIA SALAMANDER

MOUNTRAIN TREE FROG

Have you ever seen a toad that was hopping in your garden or across wet pavement after a rainstorm? You were in the presence of a V.I.C. — very important creature! Say what? You thought toads were warty, slimy, and well, sort of ugly and dull? Check this out:

Toads, frogs, salamanders, and *newts* (small salamanders) are *amphibians* (page 10), which means they lead a double life (and you thought they were unexciting!). Young amphibians spend their early years in the water as *tadpoles*, breathing through gills in their heads like fish and swimming by wriggling their tails. Natural *vernal pools* — small temporary pools of water that form from rainwater or snow melt in spring — are important shelters and breeding habitats for these moisture-loving creatures.

As they mature, the tadpoles lose their gills and develop legs, and eventually turn into miniature frogs and toads that spend their adult lives hopping or crawling — and eating insects!

EASTERN SPADE FROG

PICKEREL FROG

CALIFORNIA NEWT

SPRING PEEPER FROG

Kids to the Rescue!

Amphibian alert

Frogs and other amphibians live very closely in contact with water, so they are quickly affected by changes in its quality. If the water has any pollution in it, including dangerous chemicals from factories or farms, their soft skins absorb it. Scientists all over the world have noticed that not only are there fewer and fewer amphibians than there once were, but many frogs and toads are growing extra limbs or have other deformities as well.

How can *you* help keep frogs and toads safe? Be a frog watcher! FrogWatch is an organization in the U.S. and Canada that helps scientists monitor frog and toad populations. You don't have to be an expert — all you have to do is care about helping frogs and toads! (See Resources, page 123 for more.)

Home, Sweet Home!

It's a lot of fun to find these amphibians, especially the tiny ones (like a cute little newt!) And it's tempting to take them home with you, even just for one night. *But please don't!* These fragile creatures are happiest right where they are and will likely get sick or die if moved to a different location. Even tadpoles will die if they don't have their correct habitat to grow in. (In some areas, it's even against the law to remove amphibians or their young.) For the same reason, it's not a good idea to let a frog or toad from a pet store loose in your yard. Instead, be patient and provide a welcoming home for toads and frogs. If they are in the neighborhood, they will eventually find you!

Caution! Critters Crossing!

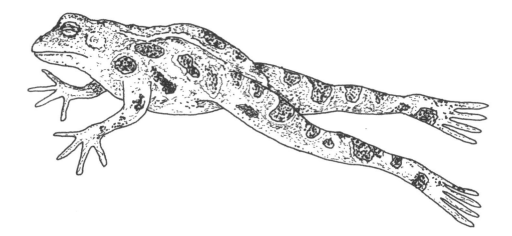

Can you imagine a toad hopping for four miles (6.5 km)? That's how far some amphibians travel from the places where they overwinter to their preferred breeding sites! Many are determined to return to the same watery spot every year to lay their eggs, and unfortunately, when their travels take over them right over busy roads or highways, it's a life-threatening journey for a slow-moving salamander. Amphibians sometimes migrate by the hundreds (or even the thousands!), so it can pose a threat to drivers as well.

That's why you'll now find toad tunnels in Texas, subterranean salamander crossings in Massachusetts, highway wildlife walls and culverts in central Florida, and frog bridges in Davis, California. These efforts are thanks to concerned folks in conservation groups and state departments of transportation, who developed creative solutions to force animals to cross under or over (rather than straight across) busy roadways in their search for food or mating spots. To learn more about critter crossings for all kinds of animals and see photos from around the United States (even an underpass for black bears!), see Resources, page 123.

Toad or Frog?

Even though you can't take an amphibian home with you, you can gently pick one up and study it briefly for a moment or two. Does its skin feel moist or bumpy? What color is it? Here are some clues to help you figure out who is who:

Toads tend to be camouflaged brown and gold, like the leaves and dirt they live in as adults. Their rough skin is covered with bumps (that's why some people think of toads as "warty"). Toads live on land as adults, but return to water to mate and breed. You can hear the males trill loud and clear during mating season in the spring! The eggs are laid in long strings of 17 to 25 eggs, like a row of beads encased in jelly. The tadpoles are black.

Frogs are greener, helping them to blend in with pond water and plants. They have smooth, slightly moist skin and long legs for hopping. The eggs are laid in jelly masses that float in the water. The tadpoles are brown. Frogs stay near water all their lives. Listen for their croaking sounds — they can be pretty loud! If you hear a "pee-eep, pee-eep, pee-eep" coming from the water in springtime, it's likely the call of *spring peepers*. These tiny tree frogs are one of the first amphibians to awaken from their underground sleep in the mud in spring. Their call means spring is on the way!

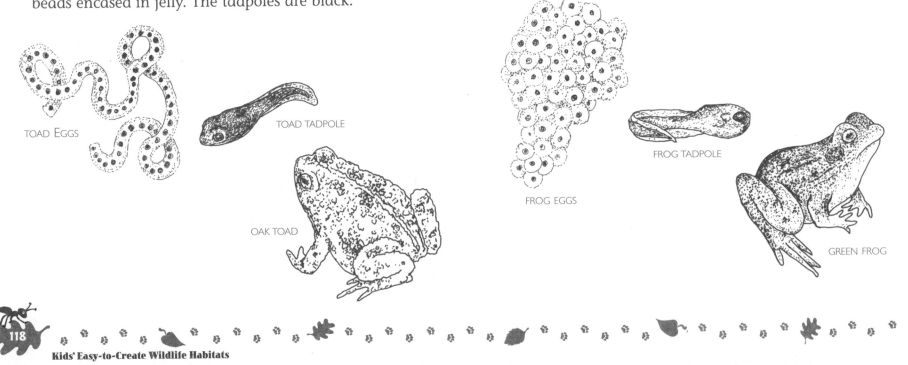

TOAD EGGS

TOAD TADPOLE

OAK TOAD

FROG EGGS

FROG TADPOLE

GREEN FROG

Kids' Easy-to-Create Wildlife Habitats

Newts and other *salamanders* have a long tail, a slender body, and four short legs as adults, making them look sort of like lizards. Salamanders lay their eggs on or under rocks, logs, or aquatic plants near the edges of streams or other watery spots. Some salamanders are yellowish brown as youngsters and then orange or red as adults, making them easy to spot in the woods after a rain. Don't expect to hear them trill or croak, though. Salamanders are *mute* (they don't make noise) and like to stay hidden from view.

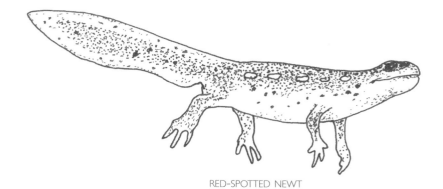

NEWT TADPOLE

RED-SPOTTED NEWT

SALAMANDER EGGS

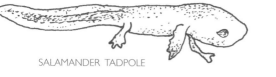

SALAMANDER TADPOLE

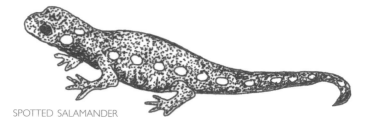

SPOTTED SALAMANDER

Healthy Habits!

Every day you can do little things that will help keep the water, air, and land around you clean so that amphibians, birds, insects, and all the other creatures can live in a healthy habitat. You may already be doing some of them. Do you turn off the faucet while brushing your teeth to save water? Good for you! Here are some more ideas!

✿ To conserve more water, set up a rain barrel to catch water from your roof to use in gardens and in your wildlife habitats.

✿ Save on electricity by turning off lights as you leave a room (hey, how about encouraging your family to have dinner by candlelight occasionally?).

✿ Walk or bike short distances rather than having your parents drive you.

✿ Recycle everything you can — bottles, newspapers, cans, plastic, even old clothes — instead of throwing them away. And composting kitchen scraps (pages 88 to 90) will keep literally tons of food waste out of the landfills.

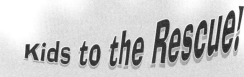

Making a Difference

Kids to the Rescue!

Habitat helpers!

Ever wonder how much of a difference kids can make? Kids F.A.C.E. stands for Kids For A Clean Environment, and it was started in 1989 by a nine-year-old girl named Melissa Poe from Nashville, Tennessee. Today there are hundreds of thousands of kids all over the world who are helping the environment, just like you, and hundreds of Kids F.A.C.E. chapters around the country.

To contact Kids F.A.C.E., see Resources, page 122.

Resources

For more information on creating wildlife habitats, tracking animal migration or participating in population counts, or helping conserve the environment for wildlife, check out these excellent resources.

Conservation Organizations & Websites

Backyard Wildlife Habitat
Lists website links by state for creating habitats, as well as links to general habitat information on landscaping for wildlife or following animal migrations.
<http://www.backyardwildlifehabitat.info/>

The Humane Society
The Humane Society of the United States has a certification program for wildlife habitats through its Urban Wildlife Sanctuary Program. *Contact:* The Humane Society of the United States, 2100 L St., NW, Washington, DC 20037; (202) 452-1100; <http://www.hsus.org/ace/12006>.

my backyard Inc.
Basics of backyard wildlife habitat creation, with lots of helpful ideas for getting started. *Contact:* my backyard Inc., 2977 Ygnacio Valley Rd., Suite 435, Walnut Creek, CA 94598; (888) 830-6930; <http://www.mybackyard.com/current/192p1.htm>.

National Audubon Society
The National Audubon Society has long been a leader in preserving habitats for birds and other wildlife. The Healthy Habitat Program provides tips and links to other resources. See THE GREAT BACKYARD BIRD COUNT (**Migration Studies & Population Counts**, page 122), too, for additional information about bird counts. *Contact:* National Audubon Society, 700 Broadway, New York, NY 10003; (212) 979-3000; <http://www.audubon.org/bird/healthy_habitat/index.html>.

National Gardening Association
This nonprofit organization has great book, online, and newsletter resources and grant programs for kids and teachers interested in school wildlife habitats and gardens as well as information on a wide range of science and gardening topics. *Contact:* National Gardening Association, 1100 Dorset St., South Burlington, VT 05403; (800) 538-7476; <http://www.garden.org> and <http://www.kidsgardening.com>.

National Wildlife Federation
The National Wildlife Federation has wonderful resources for designing and creating wildlife-friendly spaces in backyards and at school sites. Find out how your school or home can become a certified NWF backyard or schoolyard habitat site. *Contact:* National Wildlife Federation, Backyard Wildlife Habitat, 11100 Wildlife Center Dr., Reston, VA 20190-5362; (800) 822-9919; <http://www.nwf.org/backyardwildlifehabitat/>. For schoolyard habitats, check <http://www.nwf.org/schoolyardhabitats/>. See also FROGWATCH USA (**Migration Studies & Population Counts**, page 123).

Partners in Amphibian and Reptile Conservation (PARC)
<http://www.parcplace.org/>.

Wildlife Habitat Council
The Wildlife Habitat Council works with the Natural Resources Conservation Service (<http://www.nrcs.usda.gov/feature/backyard/>) and the National Association of Conservation Districts (<http://www.nacdnet.org/pubaff/backyard.htm>) on the Backyard Conservation Project. For a free copy of the Backyard Conservation booklet, call the Wildlife Habitat Council at (888) LAND-CARE, write to Wildlife Habitat Council, 8737 Colesville Rd., Suite 800, Silver Spring, MD 20910, or check online at <http://www.wildlifehc.org/managementtools/backyard.cfm>.

Environmental Activism

Kids F.A.C.E. (For a Clean Environment)

Kids F.A.C.E, P.O. Box 158254, Nashville, TN 37215; <www.kidsface.org>.

Field Guides & Reference Books

Two excellent beginning field guides with clear photos (Audubon) or illustrations (Peterson) and helpful tips on making field identifications.

National Audubon Society First Field Guides, Scholastic Inc. Available in Amphibians, Birds, Insects, Mammals, Reptiles, Trees, Wildflowers, and more.

Peterson First Guides, Houghton Mifflin Co. Available in Birds, Butterflies/Moths, Caterpillars, Forests, Insects, Mammals, Reptiles and Amphibians, Trees, Urban Wildlife, Wildflowers, and more.

Other books

Garden Fun! by Vicky Congdon (Williamson Books, 2002)

Hands-On Nature: Information and Activities for Exploring the Environment with Children edited by Jenepher Lingelbach. A great resource for parents and educators, developed and published by the Vermont Institute of Natural Science, Woodstock, Vermont. Also check out the VINS website at <http://www.vinsweb.org/>.

The Kids' Nature Book by Susan Milord (Williamson Books, 1996)

The Kids' Wildlife Book by Warner Shedd (Williamson Books, 1994)

Make Your Own Birdhouses & Feeders by Robyn Haus (Williamson Books, 2001)

Monarch Magic! by Lynn M. Rosenblatt (Williamson Books, 1998)

Schoolyard Mosaics: Designing Gardens and Habitats by the National Gardening Association, 2002 (see address on page 121).

Summer Fun! by Susan Williamson (Williamson Books, 1999)

Migration Studies & Population Counts

Journey North

Journey North "engages students in a global study of wildlife migration and seasonal change." Excellent resource for all sorts of wildlife migration and counting. *Contact:* Journey North, 125 North First St., Minneapolis, MN 55401; <http://www.learner.org/jnorth/>.

Bats

Bat Conservation International (BCI)

Participate in the North American Bat Research Project. Also a great source for bat-house building details. *Contact:* Bat Conservation International, P.O. Box 162603, Austin, TX 78716; (512) 327-9721; <www.batcon.org>.

Birds

Christmas Bird Count

This one-day early winter bird tally is taken throughout the U.S. and Canada and in parts of Central and South America every year. Groups of birders choose a day on or between December 14 and January 5 to count all the birds in their areas. The count has been happening once a year for more than 100 years! *Contact:* Christmas Bird Count, National Audubon Society, 700 Broadway, New York, NY 10003; (212) 979-3000; <www.audubon.org/bird/cbc/>.

The Great Backyard Bird Count

This four-day count of bird populations across North, Central, and South America in mid-February helps researchers to determine how winter weather influences bird populations on these continents. Every count is important, and no preregistration is required. To find out more, check out the GBBC website at <www.birdsource.org/gbbc/>, or contact the National Audubon Society (see CHRISTMAS BIRD COUNT, above).

Project FeederWatch

A winter-long count of birds that visit feeders (like yours!) throughout North America. Anyone can join in (you and a friend, your family, school, church group). You set up a bird count every two weeks and report your findings to the researchers at the Cornell Lab of Ornithology. *Contact:* Project FeederWatch, Cornell Lab of Ornithology, 159 Sapsucker Woods Rd., Ithaca, NY 14850; (800) 843-BIRD; <http://www.birds.cornell.edu/pfw/>.

Butterflies

Monarch Watch

Run by the University of Kansas, this organization is dedicated to the conservation of, research on, and public education about monarch butterflies. *Contact:* Monarch Watch, University of Kansas, Entomology Program, 1200 Sunnyside Ave., Lawrence, KS 66045-7534; (888) TAGGING or (785) 864-4441; <www.monarchwatch.org>.

Frog populations & habitat monitoring
FrogWatch USA
<http://www.nwf.org/frogwatchUSA/> and in Canada at
<http://www.cnf.ca/frog/>
These programs are for long-term monitoring of frog and toad populations. The U.S. one is managed by the National Wildlife Federation (see **Conservation Organizations & Websites**, page 121) in partnership with the United States Geological Survey.

Here are other good websites to help you learn more about the amphibians in your area and how to protect them:
<http://www.ucmp.berkeley.edu/vertebrates/tetrapods/amphiblh.html>
<http://www.frogweb.gov/index.html>
<http://www.nbii.gov/disciplines/herps/amphibians/checklists.html>
<http://www.exploratorium.edu/frogs/>

Wildlife crossings
Learn more about regional efforts to help migrating animals cross busy roads or travel safely through other dangerous areas.
<http://www.fhwa.dot.gov/environment/wildlifecrossings/>
<http://www.fhwa.dot.gov/environment/wildlifeprotection/index.cfm>

Mealworms
Mealworms, caterpillars, grubs, and other treats for insect-eating birds. Plus, various seed mixes, suet cakes, many styles of bird feeders, birdbaths, and more.
Audubon Workshop, (513) 354-1485;
<www.AudubonWorkshop.com>.
Duncraft, (800) 593-5656, <www.duncraft.com>.
Gardeners' Supply, (888) 833-1412; <www.gardeners.com .

Nesting Box Plans
Bat house
(see BAT CONSERVATION INTERNATIONAL, **Migration Studies & Population Counts**, page 122)

Birdhouses
Oklahoma Department of Wildlife Conservation, 1801 North Lincoln, Oklahoma City, OK 73105;
<http://www.npwrc.usgs.gov/resource/tools/birdhous/birdhous.htm>.

Purple martin nesting boxes
Plans and details for purple martin houses and feeders, plus lots of helpful information about attracting purple martins to your yard.
The Purple Martin Conservation Association, Edinboro University of Pennsylvania, Edinboro, PA 16444; (814) 734-4420; <www.purplemartin.org>.
The Purple Martin Society, NA, 7510 Farmingdale Dr., Suite 107, Darien, IL 60561; <www.purplemartins.com>.

Squirrel nesting box
Plans for building a squirrel nesting box, as well as for other nesting boxes, birdhouses, bird feeders.
<http://www.conservation.state.mo.us/nathis/woodwork/>.

Plant Resources
Lady Bird Johnson Wildflower Center
Information on landscaping with wildflowers.
Contact: **Lady Bird Johnson Wildflower Center**, 4801 La Crosse Ave., Austin, TX 78739; (512) 292-4100; <http://www.wildflower.org/>.

National Gardening Association
<http://www.garden.org> and <http://www.kidsgardening.com>
(see **Conservation Organizations & Websites**, page 121)

Red Wiggler Worms & Worm Composting Supplies
Cape Cod Worm Farm, 30 Center Ave., Buzzards Bay, MA 02532; (508) 759-5664;
<http://members.aol.com/capeworms/private/wormhome.htm>.
Happy D Ranch, P.O. Box 3001, Visalia, CA 93278; (888) 989-1558 <www.happydranch.com>.

West Nile Virus Controls
Nontoxic mosquito larvicides, pumps, sprayers, and water agitators for birdbaths.
Duncraft, (800) 593-5656, <www.duncraft.com>.
Gardeners' Supply, (888) 833-1412; <www.gardeners.com>.

Index

More Good Books from Williamson Publishing

If you enjoyed using *Kids' Easy-to-Create Wildlife Habitats*, you may be interested in our other books for kids of all ages who care about nature, the environment, birds, sea life, gardening, the outdoors, and animals. Plus we have many other books of interest on other subjects. All of the books listed here are $12.95, 120 to 144 pages, and fully illustrated, unless otherwise noted. To order, please see the last page.

. . . .

40 KNOTS TO KNOW
Hitches, Loops, Bends & Bindings
by Emily Stetson, 64 pages, $8.95

Dr. Toy 100 Best Children's Products
Dr. Toy 10 Best Socially Responsible Products
MAKE YOUR OWN BIRDHOUSES & FEEDERS
by Robyn Haus, 64 pages, $8.95

GARDEN FUN!
Indoors & Out; In Pots & Small Spots
by Vicky Congdon, 64 pages, $8.95

Parents' Choice Silver Honor Award
Awesome OCEAN SCIENCE!
Investigating the Secrets of the Underwater World
by Cindy A. Littlefield

Parents' Choice Recommended
THE KIDS' BOOK OF WEATHER FORECASTING
Build a Weather Station, "Read" the Sky & Make Predictions!
with meteorologist Mark Breen and Kathleen Friestad

Parents' Choice Gold Award
Dr. Toy Best Vacation Product
THE KIDS' NATURE BOOK
365 Indoor/Outdoor Activities & Experiences
by Susan Milord

Parents' Choice Honor Award
THE KIDS' NATURAL HISTORY BOOK
Making Dinos, Fossils, Mammoths & More
by Judy Press

THE KIDS' WILDLIFE BOOK
Exploring Animal Worlds Through Indoor/Outdoor Experiences
by Warner Shedd

Parents' Choice Approved
Dr. Toy Best Vacation Product
KIDS GARDEN!
The Anytime, Anyplace Guide to Sowing & Growing Fun
by Avery Hart and Paul Mantell

American Bookseller Pick of the Lists
Parents' Choice Approved
SUMMER FUN!
60 Activities for a Kid-Perfect Summer
by Susan Williamson

Teachers' Choice Award
GEOLOGY ROCKS!
50 Hands-On Activities to Explore the Earth
by Cindy Blobaum, 96 pages

Parents' Choice Honor Award
Skipping Stones Ecology & Nature Award
MONARCH MAGIC!
Butterfly Activities & Nature Discoveries
by Lynn M. Rosenblatt, 96 full-color pages, $12.95

Parents' Choice Approved
Benjamin Franklin Best Multicultural Book Award
TALES OF THE SHIMMERING SKY
Ten Global Folktales with Activities
by Susan Milord, 96 pages, full color, $14.95

Storytelling World Honor Award
BIRD TALES
from Near and Far
by Susan Milord, 96 pages, full color, $14.95

Parents' Choice Approved
Parent's Guide Children's Media Award
KIDS' PUMPKIN PROJECTS
Planting & Harvest Fun
by Deanna F. Cook, 96 pages, $8.95

American Bookseller Pick of the Lists
Skipping Stones Nature & Ecology Honor Award
EcoArt!
Earth-Friendly Art & Craft Experiences
for 3- to 9-Year-Olds
by Laurie Carlson

Benjamin Franklin Best Education/Teaching
Gold Award
Parent's Guide Children's Media Award
HAND-PRINT ANIMAL ART
by Carolyn Carreiro, full color, $14.95

Little Hands® Sea Life Art & Activities
Creative Learning Experiences for 3- to
7-Year-Olds
by Judy Press

Parents' Choice Gold Award
FUN WITH MY 5 SENSES
Activities to Build Learning Readiness
by Sarah A. Williamson, for 3- to
7-Year-Olds

GREAT GAMES!
Ball, Board, Quiz & Word,
Indoors & Out, for Many or Few!
by Sam Taggar

American Institute of Physics Science Writing
Award
Early Childhood News Directors' Choice Award
SCIENCE PLAY!
Beginning Discoveries for 2- to
6-Year-Olds
by Jill Frankel Hauser

Parents' Choice Recommended
AT THE ZOO!
Explore the Animal World with
Craft Fun
by Judy Press, for 3- to 7-Year-Olds

Parents' Choice Approved
The Little Hands NATURE BOOK
Earth, Sky, Critters & More
by Nancy Fusco Castaldo, for 3- to
7-Year-Olds

KIDS' EASY BIKE CARE
Tune-Ups, Tools & Quick Fixes
by Steve Cole, 64 pages, $8.95

American Bookseller Pick of the Lists
Oppenheim Toy Portfolio Best Book Award
THE KIDS' SCIENCE BOOK
Creative Experiences for
Hands-On Fun
by Robert Hirsthfeld and Nancy White

ForeWord Magazine Book of the Year Finalist
(Crafts & Hobbies)
DRAWING HORSES
(that look *real!*)
by Don Mayne, 64 pages, $8.95

ForeWord Magazine Bronze Award
ALL AROUND TOWN
Exploring Your Community
Through Craft Fun
by Judy Press, for 3- to 7-Year-Olds

REAL-WORLD MATH for
Hands-On Fun!
by Cindy A. Littlefield

Visit Our Website!

To see what's new at Williamson and
to learn more about specific books,
visit our website at:
www.williamsonbooks.com